Galaga

Galaga
Michael Kimball

Boss Fight Books
Los Angeles, CA
bossfightbooks.com

ISBN 13: 978-1-940535-03-6
First Printing: 2014
Second Printing: 2017

Series Editor: Gabe Durham
Book Design by Ken Baumann
Page Design by Adam Robinson

For my Molly

Stage 1

Galaga (1981) was Alec Baldwin's favorite arcade game and it might have saved his life. Apparently, in the 1980s Mr. Baldwin would play the game as a way to come down from his long nights of drinking and doing coke. In the morning, he would show up at a warehouse arcade in Los Angeles and wait for the owner of the place to open up for the day. He would play arcade games while other people were eating breakfast and going to work. According to Mr. Baldwin, playing video games "was the only way I could go 'beta' and go into that state I needed to be, where I could calm down and take my mind off everything." The rush of playing video games became a substitute for the rush of drugs and alcohol. Playing *Galaga* and other arcade games for a couple of hours allowed him to wind down enough that he could go home and go to sleep.

Stage 2

Galaga is a coin-op arcade video game and a sequel to *Galaxian* (1979), itself an unofficial update of *Space Invaders* (1978). *Galaga* is a shooter, a fixed shooter, a spacy, a space shooter, a bug shooter, or a single-screen shmup (a.k.a. shoot-em-up). *Galaga* is also sometimes called a bug war, an exterminator, and a kind of insecticide.

Stage 3

Galaga was released in December of 1981 when I was fourteen years old, but it probably didn't reach Aladdin's Castle arcade in the Lansing Mall until early 1982 when I was fifteen years old. It was a difficult time in my life and going to the arcade any chance I got was a good excuse to get out of an abusive household. *Galaga* was my longest quarter and I could almost always set the daily high score in any arcade. Playing that video game gave me a way to space out and let me forget about the rest of my life. *Galaga* was *my* game and it might have saved my life too.

Stage 4

Many consider *Galaga* the first arcade game sequel. *Ms. Pac-Man* (1981) preceded *Galaga*, but it was originally a *Pac-Man* (1980) hack called *Crazy Otto* that Midway bought out while waiting for Namco to deliver *Super Pac-Man* (1982).

Stage 5

Side note: I've never actually seen or heard of *Galaga* being referred to as an exterminator, but I thought it was funny.

Stage 6

There are lots of playing tips later in this book, but here is a cheat sheet:

1. Get double fighters.
2. Don't do anything stupid that destroys one of the double fighters.
3. Stay out of the corners.
4. Learn the entrance patterns for each stage.
5. Clear out at least one side of the formation before the Galagans begin attacking.
6. Focus on clearing stages rather than maxing out points.
7. Max out the Challenging Stages.

Stage 7

Back in the 1980s, *Galaga* wasn't the most popular arcade game or the one that made the most money, but it has endured for more than 30 years and continues to be played on many platforms. *Galaga* is an incredibly successful sequel. In my adopted hometown of Baltimore, *Galaga* can still be played in a pool hall, a pizzeria, a Laundromat, a hipster bar, and a crab shack. Those are just the places I know. I like to imagine secret *Galaga* machines tucked into strange establishments all over the city.

Stage 8

The blue, yellow, and red alien insects are bees. The white, orange, and blue ones are butterflies. Sometimes, the bees are referred to as hornets or wasps. In Japanese, the bees are "zako" and the butterflies are "goei." Sometimes, the butterflies are referred to as moths. But one of the mysteries of *Galaga* is what the Boss Galagas are supposed to be. It has been suggested that they are birds and cicadas, but neither of these suggestions seems quite right. I checked with a cicada expert who said the Boss Galagas are definitely not cicadas. She didn't think they were birds either. Another possibility is that the Boss Galagas are giant flies. An entomologist didn't rule out that possibility.

Stage 9

There is a definition on Urban Dictionary that makes *Galaga* an adjective and defines it as "to do something really cool." Here is a representative usage: "I rode my mountain bike over the continental divide and it was so Galaga."

Stage 10

Galaga starts with some upbeat 1980s techno music and a single fighter travelling through deep space that is flecked with red, green, blue, yellow, purple, and orange stars that twinkle and scroll off the bottom of the screen. Player 1 is the single fighter at the bottom of the screen. The joystick stands between the first finger and thumb of the player's left hand and the fire button rests under the first two fingers of the player's right hand. Soon, swarms of alien insects swoop down in long looping columns from the top and the sides of the screen. At first, it's unsettling the way the alien insects seem so ready to kamikaze the fighter, but they pull up before crashing into it and then curl back up into troop lines at the top of the screen. The alien insects settle into their attack formation: two rows of ten alien bees, two rows of eight alien butterflies, one row of four Boss Galagas. There is a brief pause and then the alien invaders start dive-bombing the fighter. It's up to Player 1 to save this world.

Stage 11

When I started doing *Galaga* research, I was surprised by the extent of the game's legacy. There are *Galaga* clothes, jewelry, and collectibles. There are *Galaga* tattoos, *Galaga* ringtones, and *Galaga* baked goods. There is *Galaga* art. *Galaga* continues to show up in songs, books, TV shows, and movies. *Galaga* is one of the most bootlegged video games in the history of video games and there are also a bunch of *Galaga* hacks, clones, and updates. I love *Galaga*, but I didn't know that so many other people love *Galaga* too.

Stage 12

In a full formation, the first alien insect to attack is one of the bees, which jumps off the left side of the formation, curls around, and dive-bombs the fighter. Almost immediately after that, an alien butterfly jumps off the right side of the formation, fluttering and bobbing at the fighter from the opposite direction. Then one of the Boss Galagas backflips from the top row and somersaults down the screen. This is just the first of wave after wave of attacks.

Stage 13

Rule 34 states: If it exists, there is porn of it. After googling "*Galaga*" and "porn," I found a drawing of a naked Terezi, the blind troll from a comic called *Homestuck*, feeling up the *Galaga* fighter. I found a series of photos of porn star Jordan Capri getting naked in front of a *Galaga* machine. I found out that some people see the futuristic art on the side of a *Galaga* machine as two huge orange breasts with big red nipples. And I found a photo of a naked gamer girl with her knees up and her legs spread, while a Game Boy defends her vagina from three *Galaga* fighters that are photoshopped into the shot.

Stage 14

Eventually, some version of *Galaga* was released on nearly every gaming platform—including, alphabetically, Android, Atari 7800, Casio PV-2000, Dreamcast, Famicom, Fujitsu FM-7, Game Boy, Game Boy Advance, iPad, iPhone, MSX, Nintendo Entertainment System, Nintendo 3DS, Nintendo 64, Nintendo DS, Nintendo GameCube, PC, PlayStation, PlayStation 2, PlayStation 3, PlayStation Portable, Roku, Sega SG-1000, Sharp MZ, Sharp X1, TurboGrafx-16, Xbox, Xbox 360, Wii, and WiiU.

Stage 15

The Galagans attack in ones at first, but then in twos and threes, swarming down from both sides of the screen. They blanket the deep space with bullets as they criss-cross above the fighter, which Player 1 pushes left and right against the attacks. Eventually, the second Boss Galaga loops off the top of the formation and somersaults down the screen. Then, oddly, the Boss Galaga stops two-thirds of the way down the screen and releases a blue tractor beam to the sound of some twirly, hypnotic music.

Stage 16

After doing some pretty standard google research on *Galaga*, I started to Google "*Galaga*" and anything I could think of—including "cake," "candy," "jewelry," "rap lyrics," "shoes," etc. That's how I found out, for instance, that you can buy a *Galaga* wine stopper, download a *Galaga* cursor, or buy a *Galaga* license plate frame.

Stage 17

One of the reasons I must have been drawn to *Galaga* was my recurring apocalyptic nightmares in which my school, my neighborhood, America, or the Earth is being invaded by Russians, monsters, or aliens. In these nightmares, I had to save whatever was under attack.

On some level, *Galaga* was my nightmares transformed into an arcade game, but it was fun and I wasn't as afraid to die. It only cost a quarter to fight the invading alien insects of *Galaga*. Who wouldn't want to do that?

Stage 18

In almost any video game, a player's instinct is to avoid being captured, but Player 1 moves the fighter into the blue tractor beam and watches it twirl up to the Boss Galaga. The captured fighter turns red and the Boss Galaga wheels arounds and tows it back up into the attack formation like a trailer on a hitch. Player 1 gets a new fighter from the fighter reserve and waits as an alien bee and then an alien butterfly loop down from different sides of the screen. Then a green Boss Galaga jumps off the right side of the formation with two alien butterfly escorts leading the way and the player's captured fighter trailing it. Player 1 moves the fighter to the right side of the screen and waits for the attack group to line up vertically. A quick two shots take out the two alien butterflies. Another quick shot turns the Boss Galaga blue and then a fourth one destroys the Boss Galaga, rescuing the fighter.

Stage 19

There is a doctored photo of Lady Gaga wearing a black leather (or maybe vinyl) dress that has a blue Boss Galaga at the neckline (which almost looks like a huge piece of jewelry) and then the blue tractor beam descends the length of the dress. She looks like she's arrived from the future wearing a dress from the past.

Stage 20

Galaga was created by Namco in Japan and released there as *Gyaraga* in September of 1981. *Galaga* was released by Namco's North American distributor, Midway, in December of 1981, though it didn't reach most arcades in the U.S. until early 1982. *Galaga* can be played in three different cabinet styles: (1) the standard upright version, (2) the mini-cabaret version, and (3) the cocktail-tabletop version. There was also a fourth type of *Galaga* machine, a portable mini-television version to be used when travelling, but I've never seen one of those. Please note: The pure and true and full *Galaga* experience can only be captured when playing the standard upright version. The other versions do not play as well.

Stage 21

The rescued fighter turns back to white and spins back toward the center of the screen where it lines up vertically and drops in next to the second fighter. They link up and there's a little riff of celebratory music. The double fighters start firing away at the alien armada in the brief moments before they begin attacking again, clearing out the center of the attack formation. An alien bee jumps out wide and curls back toward the center of the screen while the double fighters slide over and quickly take it out. The same thing happens with an alien butterfly on the other side of the screen. Then one of the last two Boss Galagas does its backflip at the top of the formation and Player 1 lays down two pairs of bullets that destroy it at the top of the screen.

Stage 22

In 2009, Hallmark sold a miniature replica of the *Galaga* arcade cabinet as a Christmas tree ornament. It lights up and includes a sound chip that plays the game's music. These four-inch ornaments have become collector's items, often selling at many times their original price.

Stage 23

There is only one way to play most classic video games, but *Galaga* has options. With *Galaga*, the player had to choose between a single fighter or double fighters. At the time, it was the only game in which the player could turn a bad thing (a captured fighter) into a good thing (double fighters). Getting double fighters made me feel like I was in on a secret.

Stage 24

Before I started playing video games like *Galaga*, I played board games like *Candy Land*, *Battleship*, *Life*, *Clue*, *Masterpiece*, and *Monopoly*. I played card games like Crazy Eights, Rummy, and War. I played a lot of baseball, basketball, football, and kickball at school, in organized leagues, and in the neighborhood. At home, we often played tag, freeze tag, something we called Spud, and something else we called Gorilla, Gorilla. I always wanted to be playing some kind of game. The terrible stuff happened when I wasn't playing games.

Stage 25

There are just a handful of Galagans left at the end of the wave and they attack together—an alien bee, an alien butterfly, and then the last Boss Galaga. Player 1 picks off the last Boss Galaga with two quick shots while another alien bee and another alien butterfly begin their attacks. Player 1 slides the fighter away from two bullets and away from the alien bee looping under it, then picks off one alien bee and then a second one. The two alien butterflies flutter through the bottom of the screen, but then don't retake their positions in the formation. They continue attacking instead and the fighter sprays two sets of bullets on the right side of the screen and then the left side, taking out both alien butterflies.

Stage 26

The double fighters in *Galaga* were a huge shift in gameplay at the time. And double fighters are one of the biggest keys to playing *Galaga* at the highest levels. It's easier to aim, easier to clear stages quickly (thereby limiting enemy attacks), and the player's shooting statistics (which are displayed at the end of the game) are much improved. Double fighters are a bigger target, of course, but if the player uses them properly, there are considerably fewer instances where they are a target at all.

Stage 27

Besides playing games with other people, I played a lot of games by myself. I made up games to keep myself company. I always had a deck of cards and played different kinds of solitaire in front of the TV or on my bedspread. I made up different board games on colorful sheets of construction paper that I then taped together so I could play against different versions of myself. I played a baseball game that used nine baseball cards for each team, with batting orders and defensive placements, and little slips of paper that I pulled out of a baseball hat to determine each playing card's at-bat. I loved playing these games by myself and, at the time, I couldn't have imagined how playing video games by myself would be so much more fun than playing non-video games by myself.

Stage 28

At the end of every cleared *Galaga* stage, there is a beautiful moment when nearly everything pauses. The player can move the fighter left or right and shoot bullets into deep space as the next stage loads. There is no danger and the fighter can't be destroyed. There's even a small benefit to shooting two bullets a little left or a little right of center just before the Galagans begin to enter the top of the screen. It takes care of two of the 40 alien insects in each stage, a little trick that makes clearing each stage 5 percent easier.

Stage 29

Former Baltimore Raven Ray Lewis, one of the greatest linebackers to ever play football, has a *Galaga* arcade machine in one of his homes (along with *Galaxian* and *Pac-Man*). He is partial to it because he grew up playing it.

Stage 30

I knew I wasn't actually saving the world from alien invasion when I was playing *Galaga*. And, in fact, alien insects are probably not an actual threat to the future of the earth, but playing the game still felt important. To understand how much *Galaga* (and other video games) meant to me, you have to understand the difficulty of my adolescence.

Stage 31

There is a *Galaga* hack called *Swarm* that plays the same way as the original *Galaga*, but imposes a time limit on the game to make it more difficult. In the *Nebulous Bee Bootleg*, the main difference is that the gameplay is more aggressive than in *Galaga*.

Stage 32

I was a skinny little kid who didn't grow until my late teens. My older brother was a lot bigger than me and my fat dad was a lot bigger than him. I'm noting our relative sizes because I grew up in an abusive household. I was picked on and beaten up by my older brother. I was picked on and beaten up and had other horrible stuff done to me by my stupid dad. (It didn't help that both of them were named Ray.) I lived in a fairly constant state of fear after the abuse started and before I was big enough to fight back with any real ability to return the pain they inflicted on me. Because of this, playing games became a refuge for me.

Stage 33

The flyer that Midway sent out for *Galaga* called it a "new generation, multi-stage space challenge." It promised that "new twists, new turns, new special effects including the intriguing 'tractor beam' will have players standing in line to play *Galaga*." It was just advertising copy, but it turned out to be right.

Stage 34

There's a photo of a young Michael Jordan (probably late 1980s) playing the cocktail version of *Galaga* in a bar/restaurant called Bones. I found it on a *Galaga* Tumblr, which is to say somebody started a fan Tumblr for *Galaga*.

Stage 35

There is a family story about my dad choking my mom and another one about my dad throwing my older brother down the stairs. These are the sorts of things that happened before I became old enough for my dad to turn his bad intentions on me. I can't remember a time of my dad being a good dad. There were lots of times my dad hit me or grabbed my arm so hard it pulled me off my feet. One time, my dad grabbed me by my shoulders and shook me until my head went blank, a kind of tilt. It wasn't until later that night, lying in bed, that my brain rebooted and I understood what had happened.

Stage 36

For most famous video games, we know who the designer is. Allan Alcorn invented *Pong* (1972). Tomohiro Nishikado created *Space Invaders* and Toru Iwatani designed *Pac-Man*. A simple Google search turns up any of that. *Galaxian*'s designer was Kazunori

Sawano, and I assumed that he also designed *Galaga*, but I couldn't find confirmation of that anywhere online. For some reason, the name of the person who designed *Galaga* is not readily available information. Eventually, a friend introduced me to a friend of hers who knew somebody who used to work for Midway who still knew some people at Namco. Turns out, *Galaga* was designed by a man named Shigeru Yokoyama, who is still on the board at Namco-Bandai, but that research trail ended there. My attempts to contact him went unanswered, so I would like to thank him here for inventing *Galaga*, and especially for introducing the double fighters and incorporating the Challenging Stages.

Stage 37

There is a hack called *Galaga Bin Laden* where Bin Laden's head is placed over the "*la*" in the *Galaga* marquee and framed within crosshairs. The bees are armed figures in white robes and turbans, the butterflies are soldiers wielding knives, and the Boss Galagas are supposed to represent the face of Bin Laden.

Stage 38

If I had to be in the house with my dad or my brother, I mostly stayed in my room unless it was dinner or the family was watching TV. Watching TV with the rest of the family was mostly safe, but the problem with watching TV with my dad was that he would want to "wrestle" with me. It seems like it must have started as a kind of play, but I don't remember it ever being fun, and it definitely devolved into something else. It was not a healthy kind of roughhousing between a loving dad and a happy son. It involved completely immobilizing me in different ways. I fought back hard, but I was so little there wasn't anything I could really do. After a long time, I stopped trying to fight back (stopped "playing"), but that didn't stop it from happening either.

Stage 39

I couldn't get in touch with Shigeru Yokoyama, but I did interview a man who met him in the mid-1990s. The game designer Scott Rogers worked for Namco at the time and he described the headquarters as something of a jammed warehouse space—packed with arcade cabinets, game parts, filing cabinets, and two people to a desk. While being given the tour of the offices, Scott's translator introduced him to Shigeru Yokoyama, a game designer (called a "planner" in Japan) who has been with Namco for "a very long time." Scott described the Japanese designer as having shaggy hair, glasses, and slightly bucked teeth.

Stage 40

I have always said *Galaga* with an emphasis on the first syllable, which rhymes with "pal" and the first syllable of "California." For more than twenty years, I didn't know it was called anything else in English and I would have corrected anybody who said the name in a different way. So I was surprised to find out there is an ongoing debate about the pronunciation of *Galaga*, in particular over which syllable is stressed, the first syllable or the second syllable. Everybody I know who plays the game emphasizes the first syllable, but the second-syllable emphasis has some fierce backers. Apparently, when selling the machine to arcades in the 1980s, Midway employees emphasized the second syllable, pronouncing it so it rhymed with "bag." One argument for pronouncing *Galaga* with an emphasis on the second syllable is that *Galaga* is a sequel to *Galaxian*, which is said, correctly, with an emphasis on the second syllable (and sounds silly if said with an emphasis on the first syllable). However, the people who actually played the game started saying *Galaga* with an emphasis on the first syllable and that's why it became the more common pronunciation. Also, come on: Does anybody think it sounds better to say *Galaga* with an emphasis on the second syllable?

Stage 41

I don't remember my dad ever hugging me nicely, but he used to wrap me up in these bear hugs that probably looked playful. Then he would rub his stubble on my cheeks, the thought of which still makes my body roil with disgust. It was visceral and unbearable and I was powerless. He used to rub other parts of his body against me too. I would fight it until I couldn't fight anymore and then I would just go limp. My dad would make this horrible laugh, which made it all the more confusing. Eventually, I realized it was a sick game to him. I have always hated the staged wrestling on TV because of this.

Stage 42

Shigeru Yokoyama was a bit reserved until Scott Rogers asked him which games he worked on and Shigeru said he was the lead designer for *Galaga*. Scott told him that *Galaga* was one of his favorite games and Shigeru became excited, holding up one finger to indicate Scott should wait. He watched Shigeru rummage through his desk drawers and file cabinets until he pulled out some yellowed sheets of graph paper. The writing was Japanese so Scott couldn't read them, but it was easy to recognize every *Galaga* mechanic drawn out on the pixilated squares of the graph paper—especially the famous capture mechanic. Scott was amazed by the original designs for *Galaga* on those yellowed sheets of graph paper, a pixel-for-pixel representation of the entire game in blue ink.

Stage 43

Over the last few decades, there have been a bunch of *Galaga* clones including *Galaxy* (1983), *Zalaga* (1983), *Zalagon* (1983), *Galagon* (1984), *Deluxe Galaga* (1993), *Bugatron* (2003), *Galagon 2004* (2004), *Alien Sky* (2005), *Bug Hunt* (2010), *Insectoid* (2010), *Galaxy Unknown* (2011), *Galaga Galaxy* (2013), *Galaga-3000: Space Adventure* (2013), *Galaga Tribute* (2013), *Gaxiagalaga* (2013), *Space Galaga* (2014), and many, many other clones that less obviously refer to *Galaga* in their name.

Stage 44

As a kid, I had an idea for my own video game called *Food Fight*. It would have been a simple 8-bit game that looked a little like *Gun Fight* (1975). The gameplay involved the little boy feeding his fat dad as much food as he can, the ultimate goal being to make the fat dad explode. In turn, the fat dad beats up on the little boy until he dies. Each player only has one life. The game ends when either the fat dad dies from exploding or the little boy dies from the beating.

Stage 45

Aboard S.H.I.E.L.D.'s Helicarrier in *The Avengers* (2012), Robert Downey Jr.'s character Tony Stark points out an agent playing *Galaga* on his computer and says, "That man is playing *Galaga*. Thought we wouldn't notice, but we did." He says it with an emphasis on the first syllable, further support that this is now the preferred pronunciation of the game's name. In the scene, after a brief meeting, the agent takes his game of *Galaga* off pause and begins playing again. It's significant that the agent is playing the "Enterprise" Challenging Stage, a reference to *Star Trek*. It's a funny retro reference, but it's meta too. In fact, what seems like a throwaway scene might be seen as a kind of foreshadowing. By the end of the movie, Iron Man becomes a sort of *Galaga* fighter himself, shooting wave after wave of alien attackers as they descend from space.

Stage 46

There is a *Galaga* hack called *Cataga* in which the bosses are lions, the butterflies are cheetahs, and the bees are tigers (both have stripes). There is another *Galaga* hack called *House Cataga* in which the bosses are Maine Coons, the butterflies are calicos, and the bees are tabbies (again, both have stripes). In both hacks, the fighters are cat paws that shoot talons and make a little "meow" sound with every shot instead of "pew."

Stage 47

At home, I tried to be noticed as little as possible. I often left a room if my dad or my brother entered it. I don't think they ever figured that out.

Stage 48

Supposedly, *Galaga* is also a drinking game that involves filling a big saucepan with bunch of beers and then chanting "Gal-a-ga, Gal-a-ga, Gal-a-ga" as each person in turn chugs as much of the beer as possible. The person who drinks the last of the beer in the saucepan wins. Now I don't know if this is a real game or a joke (or both). I have found the *Galaga* drinking game mentioned in a few places, but I have never found an origin story for it or met anybody who has played it. The only way I can connect the drinking game to the video game is to suggest that the "Gal-a-ga" chant somehow mimics the glugging and chugging sound of drinking large amounts of beer.

Stage 49

I made up those two hacks that involve cats, but only because I love cats as much as I love *Galaga*.

Stage 50

My older brother would hold me at arm's length, my head in his palm while I tried to fight back. He would wait for me to get tired and then beat the crap out of me. With my brother, a lot of it was standard older brother teasing, but some of it crossed a line, and the frequency of it was often relentless. Sometimes, he would just hold me down and beat me up. Or he would hold me down and fart on me. Or he would hold me down and do that thing where he let the spit dangle and stretch until it was almost in my face and then pull it back up, except sometimes he wouldn't pull it back up. Or he stole money from my piggy bank or ate candy I was saving. Or he booby-trapped my bedroom. I had to be careful walking into my bedroom or opening my closet or getting into bed. Liquids, powders, or small objects might fall on my head. Or my sheets might be filled with some gross substance. It was a kind of live-action game to him and I couldn't do anything but lose. Any retaliation on my part only escalated the future torment he imposed upon me.

Stage 51

There is a *Galaga* hack called *Beer-Aga* that replaces the alien bees with yellow cans of beer and the alien butterflies with orange cans of beer. The Boss Galagas are green bottles of beer with yellow labels (that turn into blue bottles with white labels after being shot once). The fighter looks like a white beer bottle with a blue label and the initial stage badges are cans of Bud. Everything about the game plays the same way as the original arcade version.

Stage 52

In a cheesy beer commercial from 1982, the Schlitz Malt Liquor bull smashes through the wall of a bar and then through a *Galaga* machine. That bull was always smashing through stuff in commercials. In this one, there are two groups of men with amazing 1980s hair—the Average White Band and Tommy James and the Shondells—singing back and forth at each other. To communicate how great the beer is, Tommy James sings, "Hey, the bull really scores." It's a triple entendre about beer, video games, and getting laid.

Stage 53

I couldn't really fight back physically against my older brother. One of my few options was calling him names, especially homophobic slurs, which enraged him and led to a beating for me, but there was a weird satisfaction in getting to him. I would call him a name and he would hit me or knock me down. I would call him the name again and he would hit me or knock me down again. For some reason I don't understand, I could do this endlessly. I began to be good at absorbing all kinds of pain. It reached a point where the amount of abuse I could absorb seemed to exhaust my older brother, which gave me a new kind of will and determination. This went on for years. Eventually, though, my older brother got a girlfriend and most of his attentions shifted to her.

Stage 54

There are references to *Galaga* in songs by the Beastie Boys, Busta Rhymes, Coolio, Frank Ocean, Peter Bjorn, Ghostface Killah, Gucci Mane, Drake, and many others. For instance, Ludacris has a song called "Press the Start Button" (2009) that has a bunch of references to video game franchises such as *Street Fighter*, *Grand Theft Auto*, *God of War*, *Guitar Hero*, *Punch Out*, *Super Mario*, *Call of Duty*, *Madden NFL*, *Assassin's Creed*, and *Resident Evil*. Toward the end, there's this line: "Holdin a *Soul Calibur*, or shoot you like *Galaga*." It's further support that *Galaga* is awesome and everybody knows it.

Stage 55

Galaga is an easy game (at first) and almost anybody who plays video games can get through the first two stages to the first Challenging Stage, after which the player has generally accumulated enough points to gain a bonus fighter. *Galaga* is simple and addictive, but the stages become faster and faster (to a point), so it is also a challenge to even the best video game players. The steady difficulty curve climbs and then levels off at an extreme pace and this is part of why *Galaga* has endured for more than 30 years and new generations of gamers continue to love playing it.

Stage 56

I feel stupid admitting this, but I loved killing real insects when I was a kid. Somehow, I didn't become a sociopath and now I understand the behavior as a response to the abuse I was experiencing at the time. I would pour water on anthills and stomp on the ants streaming out of their underground colony. I would stand on the backyard patio and shoot the flies that landed on the railing with rubber bands. Sometimes I wonder if I loved *Galaga* because I loved killing insects.

Stage 57

The sound and music for *Galaga* was composed by Nobuyuki Ohnogi, who also did music for *New Rally-X* (1981), *Bosconian* (1981), *Pole Position* (1982), *Mappy* (1983), and many other video games. One of the new advances that *Galaga* made was the inclusion of a realistic explosion sound when a fighter is destroyed.

The explosion is deep and smoky. In 1982, it sounded real enough to be jarring the first time I heard it. It was an affront and a challenge to the player. It was one of the details that made me want to play *Galaga* again and again.

Stage 58

In 1977, Mattel released *Electronic Football,* changing what a game could be. It was a simple game, just a series of green LED lights, and the player could only move left or right or forward or backward, but it was amazing to interact with something electronic that responded to the moves I made. The game was compelling and addictive and led to lots of fights between my older brother, my little sister, and me about who got to play with it.

Stage 59

Playing *Galaga* is full of instant gratification and one of the places that happens is with the sound effects. When the alien butterflies are shot in *Galaga*, their digital death knell is a "wakka" noise, a reference to *Pac-Man*. There is a satisfying little "bwa-wat" for when the alien bees get shot and an encouraging "bu-wu-woop" for when the Boss Galagas are destroyed. And triumphant horn music accompanies the award of a bonus fighter.

Stage 60

Galaga makes brief appearances in a bunch of TV shows. *Galaga* has a part in a 1986 episode of *Doctor Who*, but not in arcade form. Instead, *Galaga* is being played on a screen that hovers between two Mogarians. *Galaga* can be spotted in a video game arcade in two different 1991 episodes of *Parker Lewis Can't Lose*. And *Galaga* can also be found in the background of the student lounge on *The O.C.*

Stage 61

In 1978, Mattel released *Electronic Basketball* and I was just as bewitched. It was another simple electronic game, just red LED lights and four buttons to move left or right or forward or backward, plus two buttons to shoot the "basketball." But again, interacting with an electronic game that reacted somewhat intelligently to the buttons I pressed was awesome. I played it obsessively until my thumbs cramped up.

Stage 62

In *Galaga*, the sound of a fighter shooting bullets is "pew, pew"—like kids pretending to play cops and robbers in the backyard. I like that Nobuyuki Ohnogi built this kind of playful spirit into the game.

Stage 63

Galaga appears in a 2009 episode of *Dexter* called "Lost Boys," in a 2010 episode of *The Walking Dead* in a game room at the Centers for Disease Control and Protection, and in Walden's house in a 2011 episode of *Two and a Half Men*. A 2011 episode of the soap opera *General Hospital* uses some of the sound and music from *Galaga*. And the character Shawn brags about his *Galaga* prowess in a 2014 episode of *Psych*.

Stage 64

As a little kid, I was fascinated by the mall, by all the stores and all the stuff you could buy, but mostly by the plentiful junk food—the thick ropes of red licorice that could be purchased by the foot at Morrow's Candy and Nuts, the hot pretzels at Hot Sam Pretzels, and the weird frothiness of an Orange Julius. Then, one day in the late 1978, an Aladdin's Castle video game arcade opened in the Lansing Mall and my world changed. A quarter was still a significant amount of money for me, but there was something magical about playing a video game more complex than LED lights.

Stage 65

The *Galaga* music is so ingrained in my brain that sometimes I will be in a bar or a pool hall or a pizza parlor and I'll hear the music, just a few notes, and get excited. My hands will start to twitch. I will reach into my pockets to check for quarters. I have a few friends who know me well enough to not let me play *Galaga* if we find a game when we're out somewhere. They know it will be a while before the game is over.

Stage 66

It isn't clear why, except for love of the game, but Patrick Paarhoven made a functional, 1/6th-scale *Galaga* called *Pocket Galaga*, which stands just over a foot tall.

Stage 67

I was awed by my first visit to Aladdin's Castle in the Lansing Mall. It was a Friday night and I didn't have anywhere to be, so I went to the mall with my mom and my little sister. My brother was probably out and I didn't want to be left at home with my dad. I walked into the place and was engulfed by sound: the splash of tokens from the change machine, the flippers and clatter of the pinball machines, the tokens being dropped into coin slots, the hopeful theme music that started so many arcade games, all the beeps and dunh-dunhs, all the shooting and explosions, all of it mashed together into a wall of sound. I had never heard anything like it before, in part because there had never been anything like it before. It was loud and dark in Aladdin's Castle, dimly lit except the blinking lights of the colorful machines. It was a disorienting place and I was a little shy at first. I didn't know how it worked and I didn't have anybody to ask.

Stage 68

In Gucci Mane's song "Up My Alley" (2011), he makes some funny references, rhyming "Dallas" with "Caeser's Palace," and "pizza" with "Queen Latifah." There is also this line: "When Gooch was playin' trafficker ni**as was playin' *Galaga*." Gucci Mane then slant-rhymes *Galaga* wtih "spectacular" and "white rectangulars," which is difficult to not admire.

Stage 69

There is a hack called *Galaga X* for the game *1942*, which is a vertical shmup like *Galaga*. *Galaga X* replaces the World War II planes of *1942* with *Galaga* graphics.

Stage 70

When Aladdin's Castle first opened in 1978, there were still pinball machines along the back left wall, though I don't remember any of them specifically, and there were still a lot of purists who played only pinball machines and not the newfangled video games. Along the back right wall were the older video games—*Gun Fight*, *Sea Wolf* (1976), *Steeplechase* (1975), and *Breakout* (1976). The newer video games were on both sides at the front of the arcade—*Canyon Bomber* (1977), *Circus* (1977), *Drag Race* (1977), and *Atari Football* (1978). But nearly everybody was usually crowded around the most popular video game, *Space Invaders*, which was right in the middle of the arcade.

Stage 71

You can buy a *Galaga* case for your smartphone. You can buy a *Galaga* hairclip that has the 8-bit fighters on it. You can buy a *Galaga* pin, t-shirt, necktie, or tote bag that says, "Gamer Top Gun Academy."

Stage 72

1978 was the year I turned eleven years old and *Space Invaders* was released. This was the same year the Hillside Strangler killed people in Los Angeles and nearly 1,000 people died in the Jonestown massacre. A couple of Popes died and the first test-tube baby was born. The first

Garfield comic strip appeared and the Trans Am was a really cool car. The New York Yankees beat the Los Angeles Dodgers in the World Series. Movie theaters played *Animal House*, *Dawn of the Dead*, and *The Deer Hunter*. *Happy Days*, *Three's Company*, and *The Love Boat* were popular TV shows. Lots of people got perms or parted their hair down the middle. Teachers went on strike and that gave schoolkids everywhere an extended summer vacation, which was awesome. Debbie Boone sang "You Light Up My Life" on repeat in my little sister's bedroom and Queen sang "We Will Rock You" in stadiums across the U.S.

Stage 73

So many people were crowded around the *Space Invaders* machine that I had to stand on my tiptoes to see the screen. As people played and lost (and everybody lost, eventually), I worked my way through the crowd to the edge of the machine. I had my token squeezed in my hand and my hand pushed down into my pocket. I wanted to play so badly, but there were all these other tokens on the lip of the machine and I didn't understand what that meant. I couldn't figure out how to be the next player. Boys who hadn't been there as long as I had kept getting to play before me and, eventually, there wasn't much time left before I had to meet my mom and my little sister at the fountain in the middle of the Lansing Mall. I pushed my way away from the *Space Invaders* machine and back out through the crowd.

Stage 74

Sometimes, when an asteroid or a satellite or some other space debris is hurtling toward the earth, a television newscaster or radio broadcaster will mention *Galaga*—even though they are probably thinking of *Asteroids* (1979).

Stage 75

You can buy a *Galaga*-like vinyl wall decal. You can buy a t-shirt that shows the *Galaga* fighter vs. one of the aliens from *Space Invaders*. You can buy a Yu-Gi-Oh! card for *Galaga* (and *Galaxian*, and dozens of other arcade games).

Stage 76

After I didn't get to play *Space Invaders*, I found an old video game at the back of the arcade that looked strange and fun even though nobody else was playing. It was called *Sea Wolf* and had a periscope that the player looked through to see the ships passing over the water from an underwater perspective. The game was already old (in video game time) by the time I started playing it, but I was fascinated by the periscope and the underwater explosions, and I was won over by the intensity of the gameplay.

Stage 77

There are lots of people who are so passionate about *Galaga* they have tattoos of the game on their bodies. There is a man with black-and-white tattoos of the fighter and the two rows of bees across the left side of his rib cage. There is a woman with the *Galaga* ship on the small of her back. There is a guy with an alien bee on his wrist and another guy with the *Galaga* ship on his left pec.

Stage 78

There is a *Galaga* hack that is terribly renamed *Gall Bladderaga*. It was created by an internist who grew up playing *Galaga* and credits his surgical skills to playing arcade games. The bosses are human hearts. The bees are gall bladders. The butterflies are stomachs (because both of them flutter). The fighters are surgeons in white gowns and the bullets they shoot are little scalpels. When any of the invading organs are shot, they explode in a splatter of blood.

Stage 79

I was too little to defend myself against my fat dad and older brother. I grew up often being afraid. I told responsible adults in my life what was happening, but they did nothing to stop it. I learned to live with the fear and the pain and the disgust. I assumed that this was the way life was. After abuse starts, the world shifts for a little kid. I learned that adults couldn't be trusted and that nowhere was safe. But the arcade was a place where there generally weren't any adults except the change guy, and he didn't care about much that happened as long as nobody hit or kicked the machines.

Stage 80

There is a man with tattoos of light sabers on his forearms and the *Galaga* fighter on the back of his neck. There is a woman with the *Galaga* fighter on the inside of her wrist that is shooting at an alien bee and a Boss Galaga farther up her forearm. And there is a writer who will go unnamed (not me) who has a tattoo of Gallagher smashing a *Galaga* machine with a sledgehammer.

Stage 81

Sorry, I made up that hack about the internist and invading internal organs and blood splatter, but only because it'd be a fun game if it were true.

Stage 82

After my first visit to the arcade, I went to the Lansing Mall any chance I could and I always went to Aladdin's Castle once I got there. I played a lot of *Space Invaders*, but I found the game at once too slow and too difficult. I kept playing *Sea Wolf*. And I played *Lunar Lander* (1979) where the player had to land a ship on the moon using just a certain amount of fuel for the thrusters against the gravity of the moon. It had a big two-handed joystick for the engines that made it seem more real. I also liked *Asteroids*, which has that great electronic heartbeat that speeds up and slows down, but the graphics seemed too simple—everything was just an outline—and it was a quick quarter. All of them were.

Stage 83

There is a man with the black deep space tattooed on his forearm, along with the fighter, a blue Boss Galaga dropping the tractor beam, four alien bees, two alien butterflies, and two green Boss Galagas. There is a man who has a full pixelated sleeve dedicated to *Galaga*. And there is somebody who has the double fighters on their upper arm with "unstoppable" written beneath them.

Stage 84

Somebody knitted a *Galaga* hat. Somebody else tiled a wall with blue, red, and yellow tiles in the shape of a bee. It should be noted that the medium of knitting and the medium of tiling both make for great representations of the classic arcade 8-bit style.

Stage 85

I didn't know it at the time, but my adolescence (from the late 1970s to the early 1980s) was during the golden age of arcade games. There was something giddy and special about arcade games during that handful of years, the way everybody was so obsessed with *Space Invaders* and then *Pac-Man*. The arcades were jammed with as many people and games as possible. Other businesses got in on the gaming action as well. Arcade games started to appear in bars, restaurants, pizzerias, casinos, gas stations, skating rinks, bowling alleys, grocery stores, liquor stores, convenience stores, movie theaters, Laundromats, and, according to one source, funeral homes. If I had a quarter, I would play an arcade game anywhere I found one. But I mostly loved going to the arcade and spending all my money there. It was the most fun thing I could do.

Stage 86

In 2007, Keds debuted their "Arcade Series" of old school kicks. There was a *Galaga*-themed tennis shoe, as well as designs for some of the other classic arcade games like *Asteroids*, *Centipede* (1981), *Pac-Man*, and *Ms. Pac-Man*.

Stage 87

During the golden age of the arcade game, there were rumors of a quarter shortage. It seems as if it could have been true, but it wasn't. Most of the arcades were re-circulating the quarters every day. Games like *Pac-Man* and *Defender* (1980), one of the quickest quarters in the arcade even if played well, had to have their quarter buckets emptied many times a day.

Stage 88

I don't think I ever would have thought of this if I weren't writing a book about *Galaga*, but the physical abuse must have seemed like a game to my dad and my brother. I wonder if they felt the same sense of satisfaction when I cried out in pain as I did when I shot an alien bee and it made a "wakka" noise. I always put up a fight, but I don't think I was as relentless as the alien invaders in *Galaga*. For the longest time, I could never win against them and I could never beat *Galaga* either.

Stage 89

Back in the late 1970s and early 1980s, many adults considered the arcade a waste of time and money. Of course, they were wrong for so many reasons. There is something about playing a video game that can make a person feel so alive, so incredibly focused and completely engaged. In *Galaga*, there is a wonderful mix of satisfaction and exhilaration each time the player clears a stage or gets a perfect score on a Challenging Stage. Also, playing video games was a way to say "fuck you" to mom and dad or whatever form the establishment took. That they didn't get it made the arcade all the more alluring.

Stage 90

There is a *Galaga* hack called *Galapede* that makes the characters look more like *Centipede* and has faster shooting than *Galaga*, but lacks *Centipede*'s trackball.

Stage 91

When I'm playing *Galaga*, there are times when I'm just trying to survive, just trying to clear a stage, just trying to get to the next Challenging Stage, just trying to get to the next bonus fighter. Then there are times when I can't survive anymore.

Stage 92

Before *Galaga* was my game, *Galaxian* was my game. *Galaxian* is no longer my game and I hadn't even seen an original machine for more than two decades until I recently spotted one just inside the Papaya King on St. Mark's Place in NYC. But *Galaxian* was the first arcade game where I could get the high score, and I was addicted to it for a couple of years.

Stage 93

This was classified information until recently, but in the mid-1980s the Air Force used to train potential fighter pilots on *Galaga*. They considered it a great way to develop hand-eye coordination and quick reflexes.

Stage 94

In 1979, I was obsessed with baseball and basketball, so much so that I would shoot hoops in my icy Michigan driveway throughout the winter. To do this, I had to shovel the driveway, which my parents always appreciated. I turned twelve years old and had a side-part and long curly hair that was appropriate for the decade. Guys who wore a lot of vests were cool and girls who wore stretch tube tops were super hot. This same year, oil prices spiked and some Iranian students took 52 Americans hostage at the American embassy in

Tehran. The Sony Walkman debuted and Trivial Pursuit was released. *M*A*S*H*, *Dallas*, *Taxi*, and *Diff'rent Strokes* were the most popular TV shows. McDonald's unveiled the Happy Meal. Donna Summer's "Bad Girls" played on the radio repeatedly and my older brother went around singing Rod Stewart's "Da Ya Think I'm Sexy?" The most popular games in the arcade were *Space Invaders* (still), *Asteroids*, *Galaxian*, and *Lunar Lander*.

Stage 95

I just made that up about the Air Force using *Galaga* to train potential fighter pilots.

Stage 96

Galaxian is a space shooter that was designed to be an update of *Space Invaders*. The deep space had colored stars and planets scrolling by instead of a simple black background. *Galaxian*'s screen was filled with an alien armada, just like *Space Invaders*, but now it was in color. *Galaxian* was the first game with true RGB color graphics instead of transparencies. *Galaxian* was also the first space shooter where the aliens had distinct personalities—the blue, red, purple, and yellow Galaxians each having their own type of flight pattern. There were no green barriers to hide behind in *Galaxian*, which made the gameplay more difficult. And instead of hunching back and forth in their trooplines, the *Galaxian* aliens would jump out of the formation, out of the troop lines, and dive-bomb the player's fighter. By today's standards, the game is pretty slow—the fighter only shoots one bullet at a time. Each wave of aliens gets successively faster, to a point, after which it doesn't get any faster. As the levels progress, *Galaxian* and *Space Invaders* become so fast they are basically unplayable.

Stage 97

At times, my childhood seemed hopeless, but somehow that didn't matter as long as I could keep playing video games. As long as I had another quarter, I didn't have to go home yet. I didn't like dying in *Galaxian*, but it wasn't the worst thing. I almost always had another fighter or another quarter.

Stage 98

Urban Dictionary defines a galagasm as "when a person gets an orgasm from playing *Galaga*." It might also describe when a person gets an orgasm from playing *Galaxian*. That feeling is the rush of playing any video game extremely well.

Stage 99

Once, on a Sunday afternoon, my dad decided to come to the mall with my mother, my sister, and me. It wasn't something that he normally did, usually preferring to stay in bed and doze all afternoon with the newspaper. It felt awkward to have him with us and I didn't know if we were supposed to behave differently. At the mall, I was told to meet them at the fountain at 5:00 pm and I split off from the rest of my family as soon as I could. I walked as quickly as I could to Aladdin's Castle, exchanged my money for tokens, went directly to the *Galaxian* machine, and put my token on the lip of the machine to claim the next game. I don't know how many games of *Galaxian* I played that day, but eventually I was down to my last token and I started my last game. I thought I had plenty of time to finish the game and meet my family at the fountain, but something happened as I played my last game of *Galaxian* that day, and I had a breakthrough. I never got trapped under the sweep of attacking Galaxians that criss-crossed the screen. My fighter flowed back and forth across the grain of the bullets raining down. I shot the alien invaders at the last second, a series of quick shots allowing me to escape left or right. I split the staggered bullets as they blanketed the screen from left to right and then right to left. I was in some crazy *Galaxian* flow and it felt awesome.

Stage 100

There is a *Galaxian* hack called *Buglaxian* that substitutes *Galaga*'s alien insects for *Galaxian*'s, but plays like *Galaxian*. There is also a *Galaga* hack called *Galagalaxian* that switches out the *Galaga* graphics for *Galaxian* graphics.

Stage 101

On the Beastie Boys album *To the 5 Boroughs* (2004), the song "Brrr Stick 'Em" has these lines: "*Robotron, Gorf*, and *Galaga* / I got the sexy *Dig Dug* calendar." It's a song full of funny throwback references and another strange *Galaga* slant rhyme.

Stage 102

That Sunday afternoon, I didn't stop playing when my sister came into the arcade and told me it was time to go. I didn't stop playing when she came in a second time either. Then my dad came in and told me it was time to go. While I kept playing, I explained that I was working on the high score—and not just the high score for the machine that day, but my all-time high score. Of course, my dad didn't understand what a rare event this was. He told me it was time to go, but I kept playing even though I knew it would lead to physical pain. He jostled my arm, which was a super-dickish thing to do to somebody playing a video game, and almost caused me to lose a fighter. I gave him a quick angry look, and then my dad placed his hand on my shoulder near my neck—in a way that could have looked loving in a fatherly way—and he squeezed really hard with just a finger and thumb (his version of the Vulcan death grip). My whole body seized up and my fat dad pulled my mostly limp body away from the *Galaxian* machine, out of the arcade, and out into the bright light of the Lansing Mall.

Stage 103

There is a *Galaga* bootleg called *Fantastic* or the *Brazilian Galaga Bootleg*. Apparently, this version of *Galaga* was converted from *Galaxian* hardware by Taito do Brazil and released as *Fantastic* in Brazil. The colors are different. The bees' wings are pink instead of blue. The butterflies' wings are light blue instead of orange. The Boss Galagas are yellow instead of green, and, then, after they are shot once, pink instead of blue.

Stage 104

I had a high score of over 67,000—with the live fighter in play and at least one more fighter in reserve—when my dad pulled me away from that game of *Galaxian* that day. I will always hate my dad for what he did that Sunday afternoon—not just because I didn't set the high score any higher, not just because it wasted part of my quarter, not just because it took away that awesome invincible feeling I was having while playing so well, and not just because I never again approached that high score, but because my dad entered what had always been a sanctuary for me and took that away from me too. I told myself that I could get back to that level of play in *Galaxian*, but I never did.

Stage 105

In 1983, you could buy your 7-11 Slurpee in a collectible "1983 Series Slurpee Video Cup." The series includes cups depicting *Asteroids*, *BurgerTime* (1982), *Defender*, *Donkey Kong* (1981), *Ms. Pac-Man*, *Centipede*, *Q*bert* (1982), *Galaxian*, and, of course, *Galaga*. I drank a lot of Coca-Cola Slurpees that year.

Stage 106

I will still flinch if you try to touch my shoulder, neck, or head. I will pull my arm back if you touch my arm and I'm not expecting it. I have a physical startle response and will for the rest of my life. It's not the best way to go through life, but I have adapted. I've grown into my body and I don't have the same physical fears as I did growing up. I'm 6'2" and a solid 190 pounds. I'm not that skinny little kid anymore. But I'm still happiest and most engaged when I'm playing video games (or playing sports or gambling). It's a rare kind of rush that I just don't find in most parts of my life. To understand why playing video games is so important to me, you have to know this abuse history too.

Stage 107

You can buy a *Galaga* key chain, a *Galaga* porchlight, or a *Galaga* lanyard. You can buy different kinds of *Galaga* coffee mugs. You can buy a set of pilsner glasses engraved with the entire *Galaga* formation.

Stage 108

As a boy, I did not want to live the life I had and playing almost any game allowed me to leave it. Video games were a new level of escape. Putting a quarter in any video game machine gave me a new life for as long as I could stay alive.

Stage 109

You can buy four different kinds of *Galaga* pillows, each with a different *Galaga* character on it: (1) the bee, (2) the butterfly, (3) the Boss Galaga, or (4) the fighter. Somebody also made a *Galaga* blanket of the five troop lines (though it has only twelve butterflies instead of sixteen, and only sixteen bees instead of twenty). Somebody else made a *Galaga* quilt with two bees and two butterflies. An outfit called Carolina Patchworks made a quilt that has a scene with two blue Boss Galagas, three alien bees, and the fighter shooting.

Stage 110

I was better than my older brother at video games. I was better than my stupid dad at video games.

Stage 111

There is a comics artist who goes by the name A.C. Galaga (not his real name). And there are people in the world whose last name just happens to be Galaga. For instance, there is a Robert Galaga who lives in New York and a Tammy Galaga who lives in Georgia and a Michael Galaga who lives in North Carolina.

Stage 112

Once, after my dad's vasectomy, even though he was in obvious pain, he still insisted on wrestling with me. I didn't realize it at first, but he was in so much pain that he couldn't hold me down as easily as he normally could. I had a chance to fight back and I flailed hard enough that I got a short elbow in and then a little kick. I connected and he let me go. After that, the wrestling stopped and I felt as if I had a little more control over my life.

Stage 113

There is a punk band named BLK Galaga from New York City. There is a rock band from Mexico called Galaga. There is a heavy metal band from Columbia called Galaga. And there is a thrash band from California called Galaga: The Movie. German artist Nils Mohn put out a techno song called "Galaga."

Stage 114

I turned thirteen years old in 1980 and started running track for the middle school team. I was a skinny little long-distance runner, and running lap after lap around the track made me think about wave after wave of the aliens in *Galaxian*. That same year, Lake Placid hosted the winter Olympics and the U.S. boycotted the summer Olympics in Moscow. I was crushed thinking about the American athletes who had trained for years and wouldn't get a chance to compete. The *Empire Strikes Back* and *Raging Bull* were popular in theaters. Richard Pryor burned himself while freebasing cocaine and Ronald Reagan was elected president. CNN began its run as a 24-hour news station and Post-it notes became available in the U.S. People went around singing Blondie's "Call Me" and I sang Captain and Tennille's "Do That to Me One More Time" whenever it came on the radio even though I didn't know what it meant yet. 1980 was also the year *Pac-Man* was released and the world became even more obsessed with video games. The other arcade greats released that year included *Berzerk*, *Defender*, and *Missile Command*. The golden age of video games hit its peak just when I was getting old enough to leave the house without having to tell my mom or dad where I was going. I could leave the house nearly any time I wanted and nobody paid much attention as long as I was home in time for dinner.

Stage 115

Somebody made a cake of the upright cabinet *Galaga* (from the lip of the machine up) that has the joystick, fire button, game art, and the screen filled with an entire attack formation. Pink Cake Box made a cake that is a miniature version of a *Galaga* standard upright cabinet. Apparently, it looked so realistic that "some of the Bar Mitzvah party attendees thought it was a mini arcade game and attempted to play it." The cake does look realistic, but I doubt the quote is true.

Stage 116

There is a Dutch deejay who goes by the handle DJ Galaga. There is a dance club in Buenos Aires called Galaga. And there is a real estate agency called Galaga in the country of Georgia.

Stage 117

The summer of 1980, I played on a traveling tennis team (not the country club version, as my friend Joe calls it, but a low-rent, no-private-lessons version), but I didn't really have any friends on the team. The next summer, Todd joined the team. We went to the same school, but I didn't really know him. He was a lefty with a quirky two-handed forehand (as well as a two-handed backhand). We were both skinny adolescents and we made for a good doubles team, better than either one of us was on our own (see *Galaga*, double fighters). We would play tennis together with the team in the mornings and then keep playing tennis together in the afternoons. One day, it was super hot outside and we were pretty tired from playing tennis in the muggy heat, so we decided to go to Aladdin's Castle in the Lansing Mall. We rode our bikes to the mall, locked them up at the bike rack, and took our tennis rackets inside with us. That's when we became best friends.

Stage 118

You can buy *Galaga* t-shirts with a variety of sayings on them. For instance, you can buy a *Galaga* t-shirt with the double fighters on it and "BFF" written under it. There is also a tote bag version and a coffee mug version of this.

Stage 119

There is a *Galaga* version of *Scrabble* that uses double fighters as the board, which folds up where the two fighters connect. The pixilated squares make obvious placements for the *Scrabble* letters, with the red squares signifying double word scores and the blue squares signifying triple word scores.

Stage 120

Todd and I went to Aladdin's Castle nearly every afternoon the summer of 1981 and the summer of 1982. You could get one token for a quarter, four tokens for a dollar, or 24 tokens for five dollars. We would pool our money together, get a fiver from the change guy, then slide it into the token machine and wait for the splash of tokens. We stuffed all the tokens in our pockets. They always felt heavy against the front of my leg.

Stage 121

You can buy a *Galaga* watch app for the Pebble watch. You can buy a *Galaga* wallet with a design of a Boss Galaga and a red captured fighter. You can buy a *Galaga* baseball cap. You can buy a baseball cap for the Boston Red Sox, Philadelphia Flyers, or Los Angeles Kings that uses the *Galaga* script for the team name.

Stage 122

I would love to play *Scrabble* on that double fighter board, but it doesn't actually exist.

Stage 123

Five dollars wasn't an insignificant amount of money—about fourteen dollars by today's value. The weight of the tokens told me how many games I had left to play. Todd almost always had pocket money and I didn't know exactly where it came from, but his parents were divorced and it seemed to be his payoff. Even as a kid, my money came from working. I worked as a scorekeeper for adult co-ed softball leagues and refereed soccer games for little kids. Some Saturdays, I also worked at my grandfather's business—doing inventory, working the cash register, being an all-around gopher. I was always happy to work because then I knew I had pocket money to spend on video games.

Stage 124

Somebody baked *Galaga* cookies that have black frosting backgrounds with tiny dots of white frosting for the stars and planets. The cookies depict various scenes including a column of bees flying onscreen, a fighter being captured, and (possibly) that same fighter being rescued.

Stage 125

After tennis practice was over for the summer, Todd and I would just go to the arcade in the morning instead. We were usually some of the first people in the arcade after the gate went up and the change guy turned on the machines. The cement floors were always sticky and smelled a little like disinfectant early in the day. It was a little sickening, but we didn't care enough to not play video games. I mostly played *Galaxian* and Todd mostly played *Defender*. But I would play *Defender* with him even though he was a lot better at it than me and he would play *Galaxian* with me even though I was a lot better at it than him. The fact that you could scroll forward and backward in *Defender* blew my mind.

Stage 126

A woman known online as Kieshar made an amazing *Galaga* Kimono for herself to celebrate her favorite arcade game from when she was little. And somebody whose handle is "melo_joyce" made herself a custom pair of *Galaga* slip-ons.

Stage 127

Todd and I also played a lot of *Asteroids*, *Lunar Lander*, *Phoenix* (1980), *Omega Race* (1981), *Berzerk*, *Ms. Pac-Man*, *Frogger* (1981), and *Missile Command*. I never minded losing at *Missile Command* because it had an amazing game-over screen that let the player know they had failed to defend the remaining cities, that human civilization had ended, and that the Earth was now a colorful but desolate place.

Stage 128

Somebody who goes by Kaden Dragon made a little *Galaga* scene out of M&Ms, which is great even if the colors aren't exactly right. Somebody else made a wall scroll of a blue Boss Galaga extending its tractor beam toward the fighter, which has just shot a single bullet.

Stage 129

In 1981, I turned fourteen years old. I ran track for the high school team in the spring and set the 1600m record as a super-skinny freshman. That summer, I played tennis in the morning, video games in the afternoon, and baseball in the early evenings. I was exhausted every evening and slept hard, the best sleep I've ever had in my life. Raymond Carver published *What We Talk About When We Talk About Love*, but it wouldn't become important to me until 10 years later. *Raiders of the Lost Ark*, *On Golden Pond*, and *Chariots of Fire* were in movie theaters and I still have scenes from each of those films ingrained in my brain. Kool and the Gang had a hit with "Celebration" and Iran released the American hostages. The air traffic controllers went on strike and American Airlines introduced frequent flyer miles. It was a great year for classic arcade games with the release of *Centipede*, *Donkey Kong*, *Frogger*, *Ms. Pac-Man*, and *Galaga*.

Stage 130

Toward the end of Drake's song "All Me" (2013), there is the whistle of an incoming *Galaga* attack, the sound of a dive-bombing alien insect, and then a subdued explosion. The song is basically three rappers bragging about their money, their verses, and their dicks. I'm not sure how *Galaga* fits in there unless it's a reference to blowing up (or imploding).

Stage 131

In the fall of 1981, my older brother moved out of the house and to a different city in Michigan for his junior and senior years of college. The abuse from him had pretty much stopped by then, but it was still a huge relief to live in the same house with only one potential tormenter instead of two of them.

Stage 132

Drake's use of the incoming *Galaga* attack probably isn't a reference to The Moody Blues song "Your Wildest Dreams" (1986), which opens with the sound of an incoming alien attack from *Galaga*.

Stage 133

One day, Todd and I walked into Aladdin's Castle, and the demo mode on a new machine attracted our attention. The game looked at once new and familiar and it was obvious it was related to *Galaxian*. We approached the *Galaga* machine and watched the demo of a Boss Galaga flying down and laying out the tractor beam to capture the fighter. Todd grabbed the joystick and tried to play the game, which, surprisingly, it let him do. He moved the fighter left and right as he shot at the alien insects. He shot the Boss Galaga and some of the alien insects froze. We thought he had broken the machine, but it turns out that is just what the demo mode does if the player shoots the Boss Galaga. If the player lets the fighter get captured in the tractor beam, then the demo continues with normal play and the players can keep fighting while trying to rescue the fighter and finish the stage. The demo mode lasts for about 30 seconds and then the game returns to the high score screen.

Stage 134

The goal of *Galaga* is to accumulate as many points as possible, and the way to do this is to shoot as many alien insects as possible. A player can achieve a high score, but never really "wins." There are various ways to measure progress on *Galaga*—high score, number of stages, and shooting statistics.

Stage 135

There is a "Keep Calm and Play Galaga" t-shirt. There is an "Eat, Sleep, Galaga" t-shirt. There's the "Join Today. Defeat the Alien Horde" t-shirt. And there is another one with the double fighters that says, "You Complete Me." There's a t-shirt with the *Galaga* script and colors that instead says, "Get high."

Stage 136

Todd and I each pushed a token into the coin slot, and listened to the hopeful techno music that introduces *Galaga*. The screen flashed "START" and then "STAGE 1" and then "READY." I tapped the joystick back and forth. I fingered the fire button. I was ready.

Stage 137

It is pretty satisfying to clear each stage of *Galaga*. After each stage, the player receives a badge that looks like a military insignia in the lower right hand corner of the screen. The badges are numbered with a kind of bastardized Roman numeral system. Stage 1 is two red stripes and a blue arrow. Stage 5 is the number 5 and a blue arrow. Stage 10 is a yellow military bird on a blue background. Stage 20 is a yellow royal crown on a purple background. Stage 30 is a blue military bird on a yellow background. Stage 50 is a red "*v*" on a white background. Supposedly, in the late stages, the stage badges will cut into a player's extra fighters if the player has eight or more fighters. Of course, this hardly ever happens. Most people who play *Galaga* never get beyond the 30th stage and most never reach the minimum of 420,000 points required for there to be eight extra fighters (assuming double fighters in play and no deaths).

Stage 138

Kenny Kitsune designed art pieces of the *Galaga* badges for each of the ranks out of melted plastic beads. He also made melted-bead versions of both the free and captured fighters, the double fighters, and each of the three main alien insects.

Stage 139

After playing a few games of *Galaga*, a player starts to notice the flight patterns the different alien insects make. The alien bees loop down, curl across the screen, and then almost disappear off the bottom of the screen before making a final, complete loop. The first time this happens, the player assumes the bee will disappear off the bottom of the screen because this is what video games had taught us: things disappear after they go off the screen (an obvious early exception being the wrap-screen of *Asteroids*). The first time Todd and I played *Galaga*, one of those alien bees seemed to exit at the bottom of the screen, but then looped back up into play and kamikazed my fighter. I yelled out the 1980s version of "what-the-fuck," which I think was just "fuck" back then. Todd and I looked at each other, stunned. Things like that didn't happen in video games before *Galaga*. This was going to be fun. I stepped aside and Todd took over the controllers.

Stage 140

Galaga has simple controls, just a joystick and fire button, but it still requires strategy and skill. I always liked that *Galaga* didn't have too many buttons. Using the hyperspace button on *Asteroids*—as well as the left, right, fire, and thrust buttons—still seems too difficult to me. And managing all the buttons and controls for *Defender* is maddening.

Stage 141

In the third verse of Ghostface Killah's song "Assassination Day" (1999), there is this line: "UFO spot 'em like *Galaga*." The line end-rhymes with "smashed Pa" and "algebra" and then makes a slant rhyme with "Acuras." It's all about taking care of your shit with violence.

Stage 142

Galaga was at the front of the Aladdin's Castle in the Lansing Mall, the third machine on the left as you walked into the dank place. I played *Galaga* really intensely for the summer of 1982. It became my game. Todd and I would get there early in the afternoon and play until our initials were the top five scores, which reset every day at Aladdin's Castle. It usually didn't take long, three tokens each until we had the top five scores, all of them generally over 3,000,000. We had a friendly competition with one another, and then a less-than-friendly competition between us and everybody else in the arcade. It was great to have a friend to do this with—us against the world.

Stage 143

The first ten stages are pretty easy for any experienced *Galaga* player, even as the speed of the alien insects and the frequency of their attacks increases with each new stage (an exception being Stage 10, which reverts to the gameplay of Stage 1 on the most common DIP switch setting). *Galaga* gets progressively more difficult and reaches speeds that require tremendous anticipation and dexterity. Eventually, at Stage 16, *Galaga* reaches its top speed and doesn't get any faster. Of course, the gameplay is so fast at that point that most people who have played *Galaga* rarely make it that far.

Stage 144

You can buy sterling silver cufflinks of the *Galaga* fighters, dangling earrings of the *Galaga* fighters, and plugs for your earlobes of the *Galaga* fighters.

Stage 145

At first, Todd and I were proud enough to use our own initials for a high score. I was MTK and he was TAS. But entering our initials became so commonplace for us that we started making the adolescent joke initials like SEX, FUK, ASS, etc. After a while, we decided it wasn't even cool to do that anymore, so we just entered AAA, which were the quickest three initials to input for almost any game. That way, we could start playing the game again as quickly as possible.

Stage 146

At *Galaga*'s highest speed, most good *Galaga* players are playing at their very limits. The pace and flow of the game is absolutely exhilarating in those fast stages. It requires quick reflexes and smart moves, an anticipation that only comes with having learned the game well, and the *Galaga* player becomes completely absorbed in the flow of the game.

Stage 147

You can buy a t-shirt with a graphic on it that starts as the line of a heartbeat, turns into the outline of a *Galaga* fighter, and then turns back into the line of a heartbeat. In a play on 8-bit, the graphic designer calls it "Heartbit Galaga."

Stage 148

Galaga was the only video game that both Todd and I loved. Once *Galaga* existed, it was always our first game unless somebody else was on it. We would put our tokens on the lip of the game, but we still couldn't wait. We'd spend tokens on one of the nearby games, like *Phoenix* or *Asteroids or Omega Race*. And even if that person playing *Galaga* finished before we were done playing *Omega Race* or *Asteroids* or one of the other nearby games, one of us would put the two tokens in *Galaga* and start playing while the other finished both tokens on the other machine. We could do this because Player 1 can play for a long time on *Galaga* before Player 2 gets to start, especially if Player 1 keeps acquiring double fighters. That is, if Player 1 has double fighters, their turn doesn't end until they lose both fighters.

Stage 149

Even though *Galaga* is a game about shooting alien insects, it has coding bugs. For instance, *Galaga* has a barcode bug where the fighter sometimes turns into the shape of a barcode. It is not known what exactly causes this to happen.

Stage 150

Urban Dictionary defines a Galagangster as "an arcade finger jock who can spend up to an hour, if not more … mastering the game of *Galaga*."

Stage 151

Throughout any gaming session at Aladdin's Castle, Todd and I would check in with each other about how many tokens we had left. It sucked to be out of tokens while your best friend was still playing. So Todd and I always made a kind of ceremony out of playing our last token of the day. We would play *Galaga* one last time for the day in an attempt to re-set the high score on our favorite machine.

Stage 152

Galaga has a cheat, but I'm ethically opposed to using it. Of course, I can't not mention it in a book about *Galaga*. There are a couple of different methods to exploit this cheat. Here is the most well-known version. On Stage 1, if the player kills all the Galagans except the two alien bees at the far left of the formation, then dodges the two alien bees and their shots, they will stop shooting. This takes about fifteen minutes (or seven "cycles" according to some sources). Be patient. After the two bees stop shooting at the fighter, let them make two more passes, then shoot them. After this, none of the alien insects will shoot at the fighter for the rest of the game, though everything else will play the same way. In a two-person game, only one player needs to trigger the cheat for it to work for both players.

Stage 153

Forty-six college students from New York University went as a game of *Galaga* for Halloween: twenty bees, sixteen butterflies, four Boss Galagas, two fighters, and two sets of two bullets.

Stage 154

I turned fifteen years old in 1982 and when I was out putting in my training miles for track, I sang Survivor's "Eye of the Tiger" to myself. The U.S. was in recession and CD players went up for sale in Japan. The Weather Channel debuted and Michael Jackson released *Thriller*. *E.T. the Extra-Terrestrial* became the first movie to make me cry and *Porky's* became the first movie to give me a boner. A lot of America was watching terrible TV shows like *Magnum, P.I.*, *Dynasty*, and *Knight Rider*. Some new kinds of video games debuted in the arcade including *Dig Dug*, *Joust*, *Pole Position*, *Q*Bert*, and *Tron*. Also, nobody had quite realized it yet, but the video game market had started to crash.

Stage 155

There has been some debate about whether the bee cheat is an actual cheat the designer built into *Galaga* or whether it was an unintentional software bug. Many find it difficult to believe the cheat is a mistake that was accidentally discovered by some random *Galaga* player. Under what circumstances, in a space shooter, would a player kill every alien insect from Stage 1 except the two leftmost bees and then avoid their attacks for 15 minutes (without shooting at them) until they stop shooting? But it is also difficult to believe the designer built that into the code, as some have suggested, so he could always get the high score. What true gamer wants to get the high score that way?

Stage 156

I made that bit up about all those people going as a game of *Galaga* for Halloween. But wouldn't that be awesome?

Stage 157

When Todd and I weren't playing video games in the arcade, we walked around the mall and bought junk food and smiled at girls. Sometimes, one of the pay telephones in the mall would ring and one of us would answer it. Once that summer, Todd picked up the phone and had an extended conversation with two girls from a different school. I stood next to him and laughed at what he was saying. He had a lot more game than I did, and I was happy to just be standing next to him. Somehow, Todd set up a date for the next afternoon with the two girls.

Stage 158

Christopher Cantrell dug through *Galaga*'s code and posted his findings at a site called *Computer Archeology*. He discovered that there are actually four alien bees that can trigger the cheat, the two leftmost and the two rightmost. Here is how it works: As any of these four alien bees continue to attack and shoot, sometimes one of their shots is not "removed" from the shot buffer after it leaves the screen, what Mr. Cantrell calls a "corrupted" shot. These corrupted shots only occur when an alien bee fires a shot at the extreme left edge or right edge of the screen, essentially a shot that is "invisible" to the player. Eventually, the eight slots in the shot buffer become filled and these four alien bees (and the rest of the Galagans) stop shooting for the rest of the game.

Stage 159

Namco High is an online dating game created by Andrew Hussie. There is Principal Dig Dug, Meowki from *Mappy*, and Donko from *Taiko Drum Master* (2004). The *Galaga* fighter is the high school beauty queen who gets cast as Juliet in a high school production of *Romeo and Juliet*. I have no idea why the game is cast that way, but it's too weird to not mention.

Stage 160

Todd and I met the girls at the arcade and we were surprised by how cute they were. We all played video games and flirted in the ways that young teenagers flirt. Unfortunately, it was clear that both of the girls were interested in Todd and neither of them was interested in me. I didn't blame them. I was taller by then, but still really skinny. My teeth were still a mess, a gap between my slightly bucked front teeth, and I wouldn't get braces until year or two later. Still, it didn't go so badly that Todd couldn't set up a second date with them.

Stage 161

Based on Cantrell's findings in the *Galaga* code, it seems clear that Shigeru Yokoyama didn't intentionally build the corrupted shot glitch into *Galaga*, but it still isn't clear how the cheat was discovered.

Stage 162

Besides being in movies, being on clothes, and becoming collectible, *Galaga* is also a sexual act. Essentially, the clitoris becomes the *Galaga* fire button and the player uses one or two fingers, depending on shooting style. The touch is different depending on the sensitivity of your partner, but the timing and the action are nearly the same.

Stage 163

On the second date, the girls showed up with a friend for me. She was a thick girl before thick was hot, but she was also really cute and had enormous breasts for a fourteen-year-old girl. She leaned against me a little bit as I played *Galaga* and the warmth of her body in that damp, heavily-air-conditioned arcade felt amazing and confusing. I didn't know what to do, so I kept playing *Galaga*. Todd still hadn't shown up, so I wasted part of a quarter on a telephone call. Inexplicably, he wasn't going to make it to the mall. Something was wrong at home and he couldn't leave. I got the high score and asked her what her initials were. I input them for the high score and she told me I was really good at the game. That was where our brief romance ended.

Stage 164

According to Cantrell, even partially clogging *Galaga*'s shot buffer can make later gameplay easier. That is, shots from the two leftmost and two rightmost alien bees can clog the shot buffer at any point in any stage (except the Challenging Stages, of course). So even a shot from an alien bee in the first attack might become corrupted and not be removed from the shot buffer. This corrupted shot takes up one of the eight slots in the shot buffer, which limits the number of shots the attacking Galagans can have on the screen at one time and makes that particular game of *Galaga* easier than it would be if all eight slots in the shot buffer were open.

Stage 165

There is an Easter egg in *Galaga*. To find it, the internet says you must first enter the service mode, then press B1 while inputting this sequence: 5xR 6xL 3xR 7xL. After that, "© 1981 NAMCO LTD." will appear onscreen. The effort hardly seems worth the reveal, but Easter eggs weren't common when *Galaga* was released, so it still seems important enough to mention.

Stage 166

Todd and I first bonded over playing doubles together in tennis and then over our love for video games. We were a pair, best friends, and it felt so much cooler going to the arcade with a friend than going by myself. So it seems right that the first video game we both loved had a new feature that involved double fighters, which have become a retro representation of friendship.

Stage 167

You can buy *Galaga* leggings (made by Eat Me Clothing). You can buy a *Galaga* cardigan that has blue trim and blue cuffs that matches the blue color of the tractor beam running down the right side of the sweater.

Stage 168

When the alien insects are shot, they explode into red, green, and yellow fireworks. I don't remember ever noticing this when I played the game as a teenager, but it feels celebratory, like the Fourth of July (even though it's a Japanese game).

Stage 169

While everybody was still high on video games, Pinball Pete's opened up in a strip mall across the street from the Lansing Mall. Pinball Pete's had both front and back entrances and it had plastic cups to hold your tokens, which automatically made it cooler than Aladdin's Castle. But you couldn't get the bonus tokens at Pinball Pete's, so Todd and I started going both places—generally, Aladdin's Castle during the day and Pinball Pete's at night. It helped that Pinball Pete's wasn't in the mall and that it had a parking lot. Todd and I were old enough to have some friends who were old enough to drive, and that changed everything. Pinball Pete's drew an older crowd—the boys wore OP shorts and the girls wore iridescent eye shadow—and the parking lot was used for drinking and making out. I was fifteen years old, but I wasn't doing either of those things yet. I still felt like a kid and I just wanted to play video games.

Stage 170

In 2012, *Time* named *Galaga* to its list of the all-time best video games and the stub describing it says, "[*Galaga*] felt like the future of enemy AI." Of course, it was. As the player gets into the fast stages of *Galaga*, the artificial intelligence (AI) elements become stronger (to a point). The alien insects start to recognize where the player's fighter is on the screen and begin to float closer to the fighter and deeper into the corners. There is a point at which an alien insect lays down a stream of bullets and the last bullet drifts toward the fighter and into the corner, effectively removing the corners as a safe place for the fighter to hide. This player-computer interaction made the game infinitely more difficult and infinitely more fun.

Stage 171

Artist Lisa Solomon does cross stitch of the Galagans and the fighter on black cashmere backgrounds. Karey Higuera made *Galaga* pixel art out of wood blocks using 8-bit templates. Various people have recreated the pixilated effect of the *Galaga* characters out of LEGO bricks. And somebody made the whole *Galaga* screen out of LEGO bricks.

Stage 172

One time, on a Friday night, my mom dropped me off at Pinball Pete's with my little sister and her friend. I knew Todd would be there and when I saw him he asked me why I hadn't called him. He had gone to Pinball Pete's with another boy who was a year older than us, and I realized that our friendship was coming to an end. He had kept playing tennis on the high school team and I had switched to track. We were never friends again in the same way after that. Last I heard, he had become a bartender in the town where we grew up.

Stage 173

The individual flight patterns of the alien insects was one of the great parts of *Galaga* (though it was pioneered by its predecessor, *Galaxian*). The alien bees and alien butterflies move like the earth's butterflies and bees. The looping flight pattern of the alien bees becomes easy, predictable, and even helpful at times, especially when the player waits for the bee to curl back up from the bottom of the screen and take a close, easy shot for the kill. The alien butterfly's fluttery movements, the sharp lefts and sharp rights, can seem unpredictable, but this gets easier to handle once the player realizes that they don't flutter the same way twice. If the alien butterfly has just fluttered left, then the next flutter is going to be right (and vice-versa). Also, if the Boss Galaga is a giant fly (possibly a genetically altered one), then the circling flight pattern of the Boss Galaga supports the idea.

Stage 174

One of the features new to *Galaga* was continuous firing. The player can hold down the red fire button and the fighter keeps shooting two bullets at time. As soon as a bullet hits a Galagan or flies off the top of the screen, another bullet can be fired. I don't recommend using this feature and it isn't used much by good *Galaga* players. Aiming and shooting at the right time is a much better strategy than continuous shooting. Also, using the continuous firing feature destroys a player's end-of-game shooting statistics.

Stage 175

I kept going to the arcade even after I didn't have a best friend to go with anymore. I was compelled to play *Galaga* again and again. At times, it was physically painful, the way the lactic acid built up in my right arm from all the shooting and my left shoulder from jamming the joystick left and right. Something about the gameplay of *Galaga* always made me feel as if I could do better than I had just done, if I just adjusted my timing when splitting bullets or cleared the left side on the alien formation sooner or remembered to stay out of the corners or kept more vigilant about the sweep of multiple attacks.

Stage 176

The Busta Rhymes song "What the Fuck You Want" (1998) has this line: "Blast the challenger way out of space like *Galaga* ni**a / *Battle Star Galactica* cross my diameter ni**a." The song is about stepping up, throwing down, and getting it done.

Stage 177

After a player loses their last fighter, "GAME OVER" flashes across the middle of deep space. Then there's a "RESULTS" screen that gives the player's shooting statistics, which include shots fired, hits made, and hit-miss ratio. This was new to video games at the time and it was another way to keep track of how well you played. In my experience, 65% and up is usually a good percentage. A high shooting percentage also meant that I probably had double fighters for a significant portion of the game. That is, when one of the two bullets that double fighters shoot hits an alien insect, the second bullet disappears rather than continuing up the screen. This effectively makes a single shot with double fighters one wide shot rather than two skinny shots and raises the hit/miss ratio considerably.

Stage 178

When I played too much *Galaga*, I got knots in my left shoulder and my left thumb hurt from pushing the joystick back and forth so hard. Sometimes, that little bit of stretchy skin between the first finger and the thumb would become kind of raw. And knots in my forearm and tricep made it difficult for me to straighten my right arm out. Something about these game-playing injuries was reassuring to me, though. It felt good to nurse them or rub them because they reminded me of playing *Galaga*.

Stage 179

There is a way to shoot one alien bee and one alien butterfly with one bullet as the first two columns enter from the top of the screen and cross paths. If the player doesn't shoot anymore and lets all the fighters be destroyed, it will register as a 200% hit/miss ratio in the shooting statistics at the end of the game. It's a cute little trick, but I'd rather play the rest of the game.

Stage 180

You can buy a *Galaga* money clip. You can buy a wood burn of the *Galaga* double fighters with a heart between them. You can buy a *Galaga* dog sweater.

Stage 181

Besides the new gameplay, *Galaga* brought more vibrant color to those 8-bit arcade games. The alien bees have bright yellow and red stripes, along with radiant blue wings. The butterflies have luminous white bodies, vivid orange wings, and sharp blue antennae. The Boss Galagas change colors from a strange shade of green to an electric blue, and have scary red eyes.

Stage 182

My mom didn't want me to buy a home console with the money I had saved up because she was afraid that I would stop going to the arcade and being "social." Of course, she didn't understand that my Atari 2600 was an excuse to invite new friends over to play video games.

Stage 183

Galaga is considered the first video game with two modes of play—attack stages and bonus stages—and both modes use the same game mechanic. The bonus stages are called Challenging Stages and *Galaga* has eight different types: Stage 3 (bees), Stage 7 (butterflies), Stage 11 (dragonflies), Stage 15 (scorpions), Stage 19 (satellites), Stage 23 (Bosconians), Stage 27 (*Galaxian* flagships), and Stage 31 (an 8-bit version of the Starship Enterprise, a little nod to *Star Trek*). After Stage 31, the Challenging Stages repeat in the same order for as long as the player can stay alive. The Challenging Stages are a nice break. There is a relief in playing while knowing the fighter cannot be destroyed.

Stage 184

Point Blank 2 (2008) contains a handful of *Galaga* Challenging Stages in which the player must shoot a certain number of alien insects before moving on to the next level. You can also play *Galaga* Challenging Stages as a side game while the Playstation video game *Tekken* (1995) loads. If the player clears all eight *Galaga* Challenging Stages with a "PERFECT!" score each time, then it unlocks a blue character named Devil Kazuya.

Stage 185

Clearing the first Challenging Stage without missing any of the 40 alien insects is worth over 20,000 points—a special 10,000-point bonus for a perfect stage, plus the bonus points for each of the five cleared waves, plus the points for each of the 40 Galagans (and every Challenging Stage after the first one is worth even more points than that).

Stage 186

I bought the wood veneer version of the Atari 2600 and I collected as many of the game cartridges as I could. I could play a longer game on *Space Invaders* (1980) and *Asteroids* (1981) for the 2600 than the arcade versions, but the joystick wasn't responsive enough to play an arcade-like game of *Pac-Man* (1982) on the 2600. *Galaxian* for Atari 2600 was released in 1983, but it was slow and frustrating after playing *Galaga* in the arcade.

Stage 187

The Challenging Stages are all about adding as many points as possible to the player's score. One of the easiest tips for scoring high during the Challenging Stages is to use the numbers of the high score to aim at the alien insects. If the player is using double fighters, the left bullet should pass between the second digit and the third digit in the high score (assuming a six-digit high score). This method works for the first two Challenging Stages: Stage 3 with the bees and Stage 7 with the butterflies. The other six Challenging Stages require the player to move the fighter(s) to get a perfect score.

Stage 188

Nicole Grgas made a *Galaga* cake for Tony Flynn's 40th birthday. Somebody else made a *Galaga* chocolate cake for somebody's 27th birthday. Somebody else made *Galaga* cupcakes with a different character on each cupcake.

Stage 189

Instead of the numbered high score, the player can use the letters in "HIGH SCORE" to line up the double fighters for the first two Challenging Stages. If the double fighters are centered, the left bullet goes through the second "*H*" and the right bullet through the "*S.*" If the double fighters are centered, the player can simply hold the fire button down (one of the few times the continuous firing option is helpful). The player shouldn't miss any of the Galagans with this set up, but if that happens, then there is another chance to shoot them as they retreat toward the top of the screen.

Stage 190

I played so many games on my Atari 2600 that I wore out the controllers and had to buy new ones. I loved the endlessly streaming white road markers of *Night Driver* (1978) and the simple 8-bit *Indy 500* (1977), especially the ice racing variations where the car slid around corners and made it feel like you were racing in a movie. I played *Haunted House* (1982) over and over even though I knew exactly where all the pieces that had to be collected were. I loved the early Activision games like *Pitfall!* (1982) and *Kaboom!* (1982) that were so compelling and addictive. I played *E.T. the Extra-Terrestrial* (1982) even though it was a terrible game, and I played *Raiders of the Lost Ark* (1982) hundreds and hundreds of times because I loved that movie too.

Stage 191

On *Galaga*, the scoring for Player 1 only registers six digits, so the highest possible score is 999,990 before the counter rolls over to zero. Apparently, Namco never expected anybody to score that high. That said, for some reason, Player 2 can show a seven digit score of over 1,000,000 and as much as 9,999,990.

Stage 192

Artist Hiroshi Yokoyama created a *Galaga* model fighter kit for the Japanese company Wave. It isn't a representation of the pixilated *Galaga*. Instead, the model is a sleek homage. You can even buy a second model that snaps together with the first model to create double fighters. Each model fighter will cost about 50 dollars, though, so I suggest playing 200 games of *Galaga* instead of buying the model.

Stage 193

Besides playing double fighters, the most important thing to know about playing *Galaga* is the entrance patterns of the alien insects. Knowing them allows the player to shoot as many Galagans as possible while they enter and set up in their troop lines. The player gets double points for shooting the alien insects as they enter the screen, so it's a good way to score max points. More importantly, having fewer attacking alien insects in the formation is the best way to survive each stage and move on to the next one.

Stage 194

Sometimes, my dad wanted to play the Atari 2600 with me and when he did he always wanted to play the simple 8-bit game *Outlaw* (1976) or the really noisy *Video Pinball* (1981). Those were the only two games he could play—the rest were too complicated for him—and I loved crushing him at them.

Stage 195

There are always fives waves of alien insects that enter and set up in troop lines. The first thing to remember about entrance patterns is that they begin the same way for each stage: Two lines of alien insects from the top of the screen, the alien bees just left of center and the alien butterflies just right of center.

Stage 196

In the Odd Future song "Oldie" (2012), there is this line: "Get me a Persian rug where the center looks like *Galaga*." The lyric is making fun of a Kanye West tweet where he agonizes about not being able "to get a simple Persian rug with cherub imagery." I like the line as a joke, but even more than that I wish the Persian rug with a *Galaga* medallion actually existed.

Stage 197

The first stage after each Challenging Stage (except Stage 4) has the same entrance pattern for the five waves. After the first wave from the top of the screen, the second wave is a single line of alien butterflies and Boss Galagas from the bottom left side of the screen. The third wave is a single line of alien butterflies from the bottom right side. The fourth wave is a single line of alien bees from just left of center at the top of the screen and the fifth wave is the same thing from just right of center at the top of the screen.

Stage 198

In 1982, my fat dad switched jobs and had to travel a lot for work, which meant he mostly wasn't at home during the week and often slept away most of the weekends when he was at home. His sleepiness seemed to dull his desire to inflict pain on me. Also, I had finally started to grow, and being taller, bigger, and stronger gave me a new confidence. That combined with his sleepiness mostly ended the abuse. Of course, I still avoided my fat dad as much as I could. The threat was always there.

Stage 199

In *Galaga* tournament play, the player begins with five fighters, but doesn't earn any more no matter how many points are accumulated. In 2011, Andrew Laidlaw set the tournament record high score for *Galaga*, scoring 4,525,150 points, breaking Phil Day's 2009 record of 3,275,720 points. In 1989, Stephen Krogman set the high score for *Galaga* using using marathon rules, which allows a bonus fighter every 70,000 points, scoring 15,999,990 points.

Stage 200

The entrance pattern for Stage 4 begins the same way as every other attacking stage, the first wave being two lines of alien insects from the top of the screen, just left and just right of center. The second and third waves are both two lines of Galagans, one from the bottom left and one from the bottom right. The fourth and fifth waves are both two lines of alien bees, one just left of center and one just right of center, that criss-cross in the middle of the screen. For some unknown reason, this is the only stage with this entrance pattern.

Stage 201

Here's a tip from former *Galaga* world-record holder Phil Day, "Don't be tempted by bonus points on the stage. Instead, stay focused on clearing the stage. This is where the points are."

Stage 202

The goal of each Challenging Stage is to shoot all 40 alien insects, which appear in five waves of eight Galagans each. I love the celebratory music the *Galaga* machine plays after I do so. I also love how the screen flashes "PERFECT!" as the 10,000 bonus points are added to my score. This made me feel so good when I was a teenager and it still feels good today. At some point, it became my self-satisfied habit to stand back from the machine and stretch my hands and arms while the *Galaga* machine tallies my score (as if to show I was so good at the game I didn't even need to use my hands). The perfect Challenging Stages gave me the confidence to keep playing the game over and over again.

Stage 203

The second stages after each Challenging Stage share an entrance pattern as well. After the first wave of two lines from the top of the screen, the second wave is two lines (one of alien butterflies and one of Boss Galagas) from the bottom left side of the screen. The third wave is two lines of alien butterflies from the bottom right. The fourth and fifth waves are doubled-up lines of alien bees, just left of top center and then just right of top center.

Stage 204

Galaga also introduced transforms. Starting with Stage 4, one of the alien bees transforms into three Galagans—yellow scorpions for Stages 4-6, green spy ships from *Bosconian* in Stages 8-10, and *Galaxian* flagships in Stages 12-14. For the rest of the game, the transforms rotate through in the same order, changing after every Challenging Stage. Killing all three transforms in their first pass awards bonus points. If the player doesn't kill all three in their first pass, then the first two transforms disappear, leaving the third transform as the only one required to destroy that particular alien insect. In 1982, it was new and startling to see one alien insect turn into three attackers. Now games do it all the time.

Stage 205

There is a *Galaga* hack called *GATsBEe* where the alien insects are strange combinations. For instance, the bees become a kind of hybrid bee/scorpion. Also, the joystick allows the fighter to move in eight directions, which especially comes into play when the attacking aliens begin a new formation toward the bottom of the screen. The hack is interesting in a weird way, but I would rather have seen a hack called *The Great Galagsbee*, where the Boss Galagas are Jay Gatsby, the butterflies Daisy Buchanan, and the bees Nick Carraway.

Stage 206

The transforms are often easy points, but sometimes they can be dangerous, especially if the player has a tendency to retreat to the corners. The first time one of the alien bees transforms into the flagships from *Galaxian*, the three flagships appear, then two of them split off and, after a brief hesitation, dive-bomb one corner of the screen. I lost dozens of my *Galaga* fighters to those *Galaxian* flagships over the years, which is why I still take a special pleasure in killing them and getting the 3,000 bonus points.

Stage 207

The third stages after each Challenging Stage also have the same entrance pattern. After the first wave of two lines from the top of the screen, the second wave is a single column from the bottom left. The third wave is a single column from the bottom right, the fourth wave a single column from the top just right of center, and the fifth wave a single column from the top just left of center. This entrance pattern is the easiest for shooting all the alien insects, which is nice, since it occurs just before a Challenging Stage, making it more likely that the player will go into the Challenging Stage with double fighters intact.

Stage 208

Immediately after the troop lines are set and just before the Galagans begin attacking, it's a good strategy to shoot all the alien insects on either the left side or the right side of the formation. I'm not sure why, but I like to eliminate the left side of the formation and then shift my fighter back to the right side of the screen when the alien attacks out of the formation begin. This means the alien insects will only be attacking from one side of the screen. The key benefit is that this leaves small areas that are somewhat safe at times.

Stage 209

In 1983, I went to the DMV on my sixteenth birthday and got my driver's license. I could legally drive and this emboldened me. I asked a girl in my typing class to go to a movie with me. She became my first real girlfriend and I was so excited. In tribute, I always entered her initials—JAG—whenever I set a daily high score playing *Galaga*.

Stage 210

Beginning with Stage 4, some of the entering alien insects will peel off their entrance line and attack the fighter instead of taking a place in the formation. When this happens, the fighter will probably be either just right or just left of center. Abandon the center just after shooting as many Galagans as possible. The important thing here is timing. If the fighter leaves the center too early, then the player can't shoot as many entering Galagans and the formation will be more extensive. Also, leaving the center too early triggers the AI that allows the Galagans to peel off, follow the fighter out of the center, and kamikaze it. But leaving the center too late allows the Galagans that peel off the column to kamikaze the fighter in the center before it can escape to the edges. The timing has to be just right for the fighter to escape the AI of the Galagans and avoid being kamikazied. It's a rhythm that is key to playing long games.

Stage 211

If you don't already have double fighters at the beginning of a stage, be judicious with shooting the Boss Galagas as they enter and settle into the formation. There must be at least two Boss Galagas remaining for one of them (the second one) to lay down the blue tractor beam.

Stage 212

Also in 1983, the awesome TV show *The A-Team* debuted and the series finale for M*A*S*H became the most-watched episode in the history of television. McDonald's gave us the McNugget and George Brett got thrown out of a baseball game in what became known as the Pine Tar Incident. Everybody was going around singing the lyrics to The Police's "Every Breath You Take" and making jerk-off jokes about Michael Jackson's "Beat It." A bunch of movies that were at once great and terrible arrived in theaters—including *Risky Business*, *Flashdance*, *Trading Places*, *National Lampoon's Vacation*, and *WarGames*. And some new video games made their way into the arcade, including *Crystal Castles*, *Mario Bros.*, *Dragon's Lair*, and *Track & Field*. I loved *Track & Field* and became good at it if only to combine two of my favorite things, video games and running track.

Stage 213

In the movie *WarGames* (1983), the world is put in jeopardy by a real-world nuclear response to a computer game. It includes two separate scenes with the main character playing *Galaga*. In the first scene, we are introduced to David Lightman (played by Matthew Broderick) by seeing his face reflected in the glass of a *Galaga* machine. Then the film cuts to a close-up of Broderick, his eyes flickering back and forth across the screen. He is setting the high score as he plays, but it's only 58,000 and counting when Broderick, with double fighters, misses an easy butterfly on a Challenging Stage, something a good *Galaga* player would almost never do. The scene ends with Broderick letting a little kid named Howie take over the controls and finish the game for him.

Stage 214

To recapture a captured fighter, it's easiest and safest to let the Boss Galaga make a complete loop on either the left or the right side of the screen, then curl to the opposite side of the screen under where it made its loop. Wait there, let the Boss Galaga square up with the bottom of the screen (so it is between the white active fighter and the red captured fighter), and then shoot the Boss Galaga at the last instant. Just don't miss and let the Boss Galaga crash into the active fighter.

Stage 215

In a kind of meta-meta-reference, this first scene from *WarGames* is recreated in *Ready Player One* (2011) by Ernest Cline, which is a sci-fi novel set in an ugly future that has a great nostalgia for 20th-century pop culture.

Stage 216

Even as I grew older and made new friends in high school and went on dates, I still played *Galaga* whenever I saw a machine—at movie theaters, in convenience stores, at bowling alleys, at other video game arcades. JAG says she fondly remembers watching me play *Galaga*, which left me wondering why it was fun for her, especially since she never wanted to play it herself. I doubt it was the game itself she liked, but she might have liked the confidence that playing *Galaga* gave me, that sense of near invincibility from playing a game really well.

Stage 217

In the second *Galaga* scene in *WarGames*, we again see David Lightman's face reflected in the glass screen, then cut to Jennifer Mack (played by Ally Sheedy), who knows to find him in the arcade. In this scene, we first see Broderick playing double fighters while Sheedy tries to convince him to hack into the school computer to change one of her grades. We can hear the game in the background and he doesn't lose any ships during this sequence, but when we next see the game screen, there is only one fighter. Then that one fighter blows up and we are shown the hit-miss ratio screen that appears at the end of every *Galaga* game (even though there were still three fighters left when that one fighter gets destroyed). It's possible the continuity problems with this second arcade scene in *WarGames* are a reference to Broderick being distracted from playing by Sheedy, but that seems unlikely. Still, the message is clear: Video games are great, but girls are better.

Stage 218

Here are five notes on double fighters. (1) Once the fighter gets pulled into the Boss Galaga's tractor beam, it cannot be shot or hit by any of the other alien insects. (2) After the player rescues the captured fighter, the second fighter is still in play and the player must continue fighting for those brief moments before the two fighters connect and become double fighters. (3) The tractor beam is slow enough that the fighter usually isn't captured unless the player wants the fighter to be captured. (4) The player can still shoot while their fighter is being pulled up in the blue tractor beam (until the fighter turns red). If the fighter was not meant to be captured, this can allow the player to shoot the Boss Galaga and release the fighter. Or it might destroy an extra alien insect at an odd angle and make rescuing the captured fighter a little easier. (5) If the Boss Galaga with the captured fighter is shot while in formation, the fighter will make one more attack run on its own. But if the player doesn't shoot the fighter, it will appear in the next stage's formation, attached to a new Boss Galaga, and the player gets another chance to rescue it.

Stage 219

In another 1983 movie, *Spring Break*, there is a scene in which a girl plays *Galaga* while a boy tries to seduce her by giving her tips for getting a high score. He tells her, "You need more thrust." This is stupid in at least two ways: (1) It's probably him who needs more thrust, and (2) there is no "thrust" in *Galaga*.

Stage 220

By 1984, I was even more obsessed with JAG than with *Galaga* or any other arcade game. I wasn't playing video games nearly as much as the previous years, which could have been another reason why I never took to *Gaplus*. But in fact, hardly anybody was playing as many arcade games. The arcade bubble had burst nearly as quickly as it had grown, and home consoles became the rage. Some video game histories suggest that *Gaplus* wasn't as successful as *Galaga* because the time of the scrolling space shooter had passed by 1984, but the time of the arcade was already on its downslope as well.

Stage 221

There is some debate about whether the player should use a single fighter or double fighters after Stage 15, when *Galaga* gets really fast and never slows down again. Of course, it's much easier to lose one of the double fighters or even both of them once the game speeds up. This is true because the double fighters provide a much larger target, and also because double fighters can't hide in the left or right corner in the later stages when the AI gets stronger (single fighters can't either). But especially in the later stages, the double fighters are key to killing as many alien insects as possible before they set up in formation. This allows the players to eliminate one side of the formation (or even the whole formation) before the swarming attacks begin, which makes it easier to survive and clear stage after stage. An argument can be made for either style of play, but experts agree that to achieve high scores, double fighters is the one true strategy.

Stage 222

I loved *Galaxian* and then I loved *Galaga* even more, but I never loved any of the other sequels to *Galaxian* and *Galaga*. I hated *Gaplus*, especially the name. (Wouldn't even *Galaplus* be better?) It was clearly a poor choice and Namco tried to change it to *Galaga 3*—in part to clarify that the space shooter was the follow-up to *Galaga*. Of course, this just created a different kind of confusion since *Gaplus* in numerical order should have been called *Galaga 2* or *Galaxian 3*. The naming problems continued with Namco's next arcade update, *Galaga '88* (1987), the best part of which is that the player can start with a single fighter or double fighters. *Galaga '88* was later released on different systems, variously, as *Galaga '90*, *Galaga '91*, and, to confuse the gameplaying world even more, *Galaga 2*.

Stage 223

Generally, it isn't worth the risk to max out points on the Boss Galagas travelling with alien butterfly escorts. A player gets 400 for shooting an attacking Boss Galaga, 800 for shooting a Boss Galaga with one butterfly escort, and 1600 for shooting a Boss Galaga with two butterfly escorts. But that extra 400 or 1,200 points isn't worth the risk of losing even an occasional fighter trying to get those max points. A player needs to be successful about 60 times without a lost fighter to justify the extra points that would lead to the bonus fighter awarded every 70,000 points.

Stage 224

There is a hack called *Galaga '99* (which is a play on *Galaga '88*) that changes the fighters into triangles and makes the Galagans into more angular alien insects. The numbers and letters are modern as well, though the gameplay is basically the same as *Galaga*.

Stage 225

The writer (and my friend) Stephen Graham Jones wrote this list of life lessons that *Galaga* teaches:

1. The beginning stages are easy.
2. Remember where the center is during challenging times.
3. Catch problems when the stage begins and they won't catch you later.
4. Your enemy can be your friend, your savior.
5. Life is so much easier when you have somebody standing beside you.
6. You can shoot yourself if you're not careful.
7. The challenges adapt.

8. Things soon start coming at you way too fast.
9. Don't get stuck in a corner. Take the fight to them.
10. Pay attention. There are patterns to life.
11. If you stop to count points, you're not playing the game right.
12. Your hit/miss ratio only matters to others.
13. A new life makes the most pleasant sound.
14. One quarter can last forever, if you do it right.
15. Seeing your name in lights is forever temporary.

Stage 226

In 1994, Namco released *Galaxian³: Project Dragoon* and then *Galaxian³: Attack of the Zolgear*, both of which were laserdiscs that ran on arcade hardware for something Namco called the Theater 6 system. In 1995, Namco released *Namco Classics Collection Volume I*, a compilation of *Galaga*, *Xevious*, and *Mappy*. You could play the original *Galaga* on this arcade cabinet or *Galaga Arrangement*, which plays mostly the same as the original except for faster shooting, more Boss Galagas, and more variation in the entrance patterns.

Stage 227

Besides *WarGames* and *The Avengers*, *Galaga* makes brief appearances in a bunch of other movies, including *Joysticks* (1983), *The Karate Kid* (1984), *Something Wild* (1986), *Planes, Trains, and Automobiles* (1987), *Death Wish 4* (1987), and *Desert Blue* (1998). *Galaga* appears in the opening credits and the end credits of *Grandma's Boy* (2006), as well as the end credits of *Scott Pilgrim vs. the World* (2010).

Stage 228

I probably shouldn't have agreed to write a book about a video game that has almost no story to it, but I didn't think of that before I signed the contract for *Galaga*. The futuristic art on the machine doesn't tell the player much about the context of *Galaga* and the instructions mostly concern gameplay. The fighter must defend the home planet against the incoming swarms of alien insects. That's all the player knows.

Stage 229

In 2000, Namco released *Galaga: Destination Earth*, a 3D update of the classic *Galaga* that is only available for home play. In 2004, Namco released a compilation called *Ms. Pac-Man and Friends* that includes *Galaga*. It is just a joystick that you can plug into your TV, but the gameplay is slow and the resolution is poor. In 2007, *Galaga Remix* was released for Wii (as part of the *Namco Museum Remix*). This version is a weird combination of *Galaga*, *Pac-Man*, and *Super Mario Galaxy* (2007), which makes it a complete mess. In 2008, *Galaga Legions* was released for Xbox Live Arcade and then *Galaga Legions DX* was released in 2011. Also in 2011, Namco released *Pac-Man and Galaga Dimensions*, which includes three versions of *Pac-Man* and three versions of *Galaga*—the original, *Galaga Legions*, and the new *Galaga 3D Impact*, an on-rails shooter I can't recommend to anybody.

Stage 230

Still, there is an implicit story in *Galaga*, as with so many of the early arcade games. And in 2013, writer Ryan North (of *Dinosaur Comics* and *Adventure Time* fame) and artists Christopher Hastings and Anthony Clark began serializing a *Galaga* comic online at Shifty Look. They created a backstory for the video game that begins with Earth being invaded by alien insects. In the comic, a *Galaga* bee crashes in the backyard of two gamer girls (Betty Moodie and Penelope Eagleburger) who are playing video games. The destroyed bee breaks up into different colors of pixilated cubes that are red, white, and blue. The gamer girls figure out how to arrange them into the shape of the fighter. The American president tries to get the girls to give the fighter to the U.S. military, but they refuse. The president tells them, "You can't just treat this like a video game."

Stage 231

I started writing this book the summer of 2013, and I started playing *Galaga* again any time I saw a machine anywhere. I was trying to get that awesome feeling back that I had as a teenager playing the game, but I couldn't recapture that flow and that feeling. I began to feel as if it just wouldn't happen again, but that was OK: I was still having a ton of fun researching the book and remembering those days of playing video games in the arcade.

Stage 232

In the comic, Betty and Penelope proceed to play life just like a video game. Betty flies the new fighter into outer space and Penelope assumes mission control from the house. There is a funny bit about the space battle always being two-dimensional, then a panel showing two formations of Galagans (instead of one formation) and only 36 Galagans per formation (instead of 40, four alien butterflies missing). After Betty and Penelope accumulate 20,000 points, another fighter forms out of the pixilated cubes and Betty gets double fighters (though it shows the two fighters stacked instead of attached to each other, side-by-side). Betty tells Penelope, "It's awesome that we're doing this together." Then Betty's fighter gets blown up and she floats out into space in one of the cubes. She reaches the second fighter where she finds that all the controls are different. She fights on for a little bit before her second (and last) ship blows up, leaving Betty again floating in space in a cube. In a last set of panels that don't have any words, Penelope arrives in a fighter, shooting alien insects and rescuing Betty. This sweet moment emphasizes the implicit friendship theme that has always been a part of *Galaga*.

Stage 233

There is a physical and emotional rush to playing a video game well. There's a pride in the achievement of a high score that makes a player want to raise their arms over their head in triumph. It's how I feel every time I get a perfect score on *Galaga*'s Challenging Stages. It activates the regions of the brain involved with reward and addiction, which is part of why I could play *Galaga* over and over again, and part of why I still do. It's what winning feels like.

Stage 234

Galaga was built for righthanders, but some lefthanders use their dominant left hand for the fire button and their non-dominant right hand for moving the joystick left and right, which is known as x-style because of the crossed arms.

Stage 235

In 2010, Namco released a *Pac-Man* 30th anniversary arcade machine called *Pac-Man's Arcade Party*, a 12-1 set up that includes *Galaga* and *Galaxian*. There aren't many of those machines around, but there are lots of machines from 2001, when Namco released *Class of 1981 / 20 Year Reunion*, which includes *Ms. Pac-Man* and *Galaga*. Everything is the same as the originals in the 20th anniversary machine, even the bugs and cheats, except for the new "continue" feature. In *Galaga*, after the last fighter is destroyed, a player can continue from that stage and add-on to their score. This means that high scores could be made with multiple quarters, which just isn't right.

Stage 236

My girlfriend Molly and I were driving from Baltimore, Maryland to Lansing, Michigan where I grew up. We had been driving for hours and had just gotten on the Ohio Turnpike when we needed gas. I filled up the gas tank and then went inside to find Molly and get some food. Walking in, I saw a pair of arcade games next to the restrooms—*Daytona USA* and a *Class of 1981 / 20 Year Reunion* machine with *Ms. Pac-Man* and *Galaga*. I approached the machine and noticed the glass had a weird glare on it, but I slipped my quarter into the coin slot anyway, and pressed the one player button for *Galaga*. I fingered the fire button and thumbed the joystick. There was a big blind spot on the right side of the screen, but the controls felt good. Besides, the game is slow enough through the early stages that the glare didn't cause any serious problems. Then I hit Stage 16 and my game fell apart. The attacking aliens were moving too fast for me to adjust to the parts of the screen I couldn't see and I lost all my fighters in quick succession. I walked away in disgust, but there was something about playing that machine that felt right, and I wanted to find another machine soon.

Stage 237

On the television show *Lost*, there was a seeming throwaway reference, a DHARMA Initiative submarine named *Galaga* that transports people from the outside world to the island on which *Lost* takes place. Eventually, the submarine is destroyed, removing a way to escape from the island. Many people have tried to find some meaning in the reference, but it turns out the submarine was named *Galaga* because two of *Lost*'s executive producers played *Galaga* a lot during the third season. It wasn't a clue or anything like that. It was just an inside joke.

Stage 238

Molly calls these bits of trivia about *Galaga* "Kimballaga," which she defines as a strangely extensive knowledge of *Galaga* that almost nobody except Michael Kimball knows.

Stage 239

In the book and movie *Less Than Zero* (1985; 1987), a truck full of video games passes the family car with the narrator, his mother, and his two sisters inside it. One of the sisters asks, "Mom, do you think if I asked Dad he'd get me *Galaga* for Christmas?" She's talking about the arcade game. The little scene is supposed to show her decadence, her wanting more and more yet never being satisfied.

Stage 240

We now know the rush from playing a video game is a neurochemical high, but this wasn't commonly known back in the early 1980s when I was spending almost all the money I had on arcade games. When *Galaga* gets super fast, I am playing at the very limit of my hand-eye coordination. And the more challenging a game is, the more exuberant the rush is when a player clears a difficult level, which in turn makes the game even more addictive. *Galaga* was just hard enough that I could feel good about playing it really well, but never actually master the fastest stages.

Stage 241

Gerwin Schalk has used *Galaga* in research on brain implants to see if an epileptic patient could play the game with his thoughts. The patient is connected to a computer by a headset of wires and moves the fighter left and right just by thinking about moving his tongue back and forth. Through *Galaga*, a researcher proved that "a thought" can become "a software command."

Stage 242

There is a *Galaga* hack called *Galigula* in which the bosses are the heads of Roman emperors, the bees are people in togas, and the butterflies are two people fucking. The bullets are daggers in honor of Caligula's assassination.

Stage 243

I never realized this until I saw a photo that Molly took of me playing *Galaga* at the service plaza on the Ohio Turnpike, but I have a *Galaga* stance. I place more weight on my left leg, which is set back, and less weight on my right leg, which is more forward, the toe of my right shoe nearly touching the machine. I can only assume that this *Galaga* stance is functional and helps to balance the different kinds of action that are required for the left hand (joystick) and the right hand (fire button).

Stage 244

Galaga is big in Japan, where the game was first released, but it also has huge followings in America, England, and Australia. It was never meant to be a hit, but the 40,000 original *Galaga* machines weren't enough for the world. So Namco took some of their *Bosconian* machines that weren't selling and converted some of them to *Galaga* machines. This required switching out the control panel and board, rotating the monitor, and then applying *Galaga* art over the *Bosconian* art. This is why some of the *Galaga* cabinets are white with a gold *Galaga* logo, rather than black with a green *Galaga* logo. The Arcade Museum notes that there are currently 91,414 *Galaga* machines in the world.

Stage 245

I made up the *Galigula* hack too, but only because I was explaining *Galaga* as a sex act to Molly and she blurted out, "Galigula."

Stage 246

Every time a *Galaga* game ends, I immediately want to slip another quarter into the coin slot and play again. That rush I received from playing *Galaga* made the rest of my life more tolerable. There was a satisfaction in playing video games that I mostly only found with other games—especially sports like baseball, basketball, and tennis. In retrospect, the daily doses of endorphins that I received from playing video games and playing sports helped keep my depression at bay for extended periods of time throughout my adolescence. After I dropped a quarter into the coin slot of a *Galaga* game, I lost myself.

Stage 247

Different *Galaga* machines sometimes have different difficulty settings. It depends on the arcade. A player can usually tell what the difficulty level is by the scores at which the machine awards bonus fighters. The standard setting awards a bonus fighter at 20,000, at 70,000, and then at every 70,000 after that. But some machines have different DIP switch settings for the bonus fighters. On some easier machines, that first fighter is awarded at 20,000 points and the second fighter at 60,000 points, and then at every 60,000 after that. More difficult machines award the first fighter at 30,000 points and the second fighter at 80,000, 100,000, 120,000 or even 150,000 points.

Stage 248

In the movie *Gamer* (2009), *Galaxian* and *Galaga* appear in the hideout of the Humanz. In *Skateland* (2010), *Galaga* is at the skating rink. In the Argentinean movie *Phase 7* (2011), which is about a man protecting his pregnant wife in a quarantined apartment building, *Galaga* appears on a TV in the background.

Stage 249

Molly and I were farther along the Ohio Turnpike when we saw a road sign for a service plaza. I looked over at Molly and she said, "Sure." I flicked on the turn signal and exited for the service plaza. I didn't fill up the gas tank or visit the restroom or order any food. I spotted the bank of video games just outside the convenience store—one of those claw crane games, another racing game, and another Namco 20th anniversary machine with *Ms. Pac-Man* and *Galaga*. The fire button was sticky, but I slipped my quarter in anyway. I got double fighters near the end of Stage 1 and kept them deep into the game, something like Stage 28, and then the fire button actually got stuck and wouldn't pop back up. I banged on the lip of the machine with my fist, but the machine stayed in its continuous firing mode as if it were on a weird suicide mission. I kept moving the double fighters left and right as best as I could, but I didn't last long in those fast stages. Still, playing *Galaga* was starting to feel like playing *Galaga* used to feel.

Stage 250

There are four different settings for *Galaga*. On the A rank (the easiest), the game resets after Stage 255. On the B rank, the game rolls to Stage 0, which plays like a weird combination of the Stage 7 Challenging Stage and an attack stage where the Galagans fire at the fighter. If the player completes Stage 0, then the machine rolls to Stage 1 and becomes easy again. On the C Rank, Stage 0 is a kill screen and no more alien insects enter the screen. The player can move their fighter right and left and shoot, but nothing else happens. There is no Stage 1 that reappears and the player cannot die (in a sense, this is the only setting on which *Galaga* can be "won"). On the D rank (the most difficult), the machine rolls to Stage 0, which plays like Stage 1 (no extra Galagans dive-bombing and no alien insects firing as they enter), but is still fast like Stage 255. After completing Stage 0 on the D rank, *Galaga* rolls to Stage 1 and the gameplay gets easy again.

Stage 251

In 2011, Namco released the *30th Anniversary Collection* for mobile devices, which includes *Galaxian* for free, but then it costs money to download the triple package of *Galaga*, *Gaplus*, and *Galaga '88*. And in 2013, *Galaga Special Edition* was released as a free app.

Stage 252

The fact that I couldn't ever beat *Galaga* appealed to my need for perfection. After a *Galaga* player reaches a certain level of proficiency, there are marginal improvements. I never had a huge breakthrough playing *Galaga* when I was a teenager. My highest score was just over 685,000. I never reached the point where I could just keep playing and playing. I could clear some of the super fast stages, but I couldn't do it endlessly. I never reached 1,000,000 and turned over the high score. I never made it through all 255 stages and Stage 0 and then back to Stage 1. I could lay down the daily high score on nearly any *Galaga* machine I came across when I was a teenager and I still can today, but I never beat the game. I always died.

Stage 253

Galaga continues to be a popular arcade game because 80s retro is cool, because of Namco's *Ms. Pac-Man/ Galaga* 20th anniversary machine, because of other compilation machines, and because it is the best shooter from the golden age of video games. *Galaga* did a lot of great new things when it was released, but it is the balanced pace of the gameplay that keeps people playing it today. And it is also the nostalgia for the golden age of the arcade. *Galaga* takes me right back to some of the good parts of my childhood.

Stage 254

Galaga has no Stage 256. The game goes from Stage 255 to Stage 0 or from Stage 255 to a kill screen. This happens with a bunch of the classic 8-bit arcade games including *Dig Dug*, *Pac-Man*, and, of course, *Galaga*.

Stage 255

Along the Ohio Turnpike, Molly and I stopped more often than we needed to and it turned into its own game. We made up fake excuses—an urgent need for Lemonheads or 7 Layer Dip Tortilla Combos or a new pair of sunglasses even though it was dark outside—so we could stop and I could play *Galaga*. The next service plaza had another claw crane machine and another 20th anniversary machine. The glass looked clean and the fire button felt responsive. There was a tall black joystick instead of the little red knob, but it felt supple. I inserted my quarter and pressed the one player button. I got my double fighters and cruised through the first 30 stages. I cleared most of the troop lines as they entered, so just a few alien insects were left to attack on each stage. I kept both my double fighters alive and racked up lots of points on the Challenging Stages. I kept my double fighters moving and didn't get pinned down in the corners. I drew attacks to a certain area of the screen— left, middle, right—and then moved out of that area to render the attack harmless. I had over 400,000 points, had just cleared Stage 34, and the Challenging Stages had started to repeat. Molly was standing next to me, lightly pressed against me as I played, and I realized that this was the feeling I used to have when I played *Galaga*. I said, "Let's go," and walked away from the machine. I could hear the double explosion of my double fighters being destroyed as we walked out toward the parking lot.

Stage 0

Kill screen.

ACKNOWLEDGMENTS

I read a lot of websites including the *Galaga* pages at Arcade-History, Arcadeshop.com, BMIGaming.com, Computer Archeology, Wikipedia, euro-arcade.de, galaga.info, GameFAQs, GameLory, IGN, IMDB, JasonEckert.net, Lostpedia, Mr Boss' Design Lair, Racketboy, Rap Genius, StrategyWiki, TV Tropes, and wikiHow. You can find the *Galaga* comic at Shifty Look. I want to thank Christopher Cantrell, Scott Rogers, and Tim Train for help with different aspects of the research. A huge thank you to Gabe Durham for his amazing edits, another one to Ken Baumann for the striking cover, another one to Adam Robinson for the clean interior, and one each to Ryan Plummer and Michael P. Williams for their keen eyes. And thank you over and over again to my Molly Englund for reading multiple drafts of *Galaga* (the book) and for playing lots of *Galaga* (the video game) with me.

SPECIAL THANKS

For making our first season of books possible, Boss Fight Books would like to thank Ken Durham, Jakub Koziol, Cathy Durham, Maxwell Neely-Cohen, Adrian Purser, Kevin John Harty, Gustav Wedholm, Theodore Fox, Anders Ekermo, Jim Fasoline, Mohammed Taher, Joe Murray, Ethan Storeng, Bill Barksdale, Max Symmes, Philip J. Reed, Robert Bowling, Jason Morales, Keith Charles, and Asher Henderson.

ALSO FROM
BOSS FIGHT BOOKS